WRITER'S SECRET
WEAPON
Reference Guide

WRITER'S SECRET
WEAPON
Reference Guide

CHEYENNE McCRAY
H. D. THOMSON

CONTENTS

INTRODUCTION

Cheyenne and H.D. welcome you to *Writer's Secret Weapon Reference Guide!*

About the book:

We have designed this book with you in mind—no matter your skill level or genre, you can find something within these pages that will trigger new ideas to help you on your writing journey. You might have written yourself into a corner, met a roadblock, or wondered what comes next. Perhaps you need ideas to get you started on creating your character profiles, refining your plot, or giving your protagonist motivation. Here's where you can find that and more!

As writers with a combined forty years of experience, we've been right where you are. We've each had days where the words fly, and others where we've faced frustration with not a creative spark in sight. At some point all of us find ourselves staring at a page, needing some kind of idea to help us move forward. Maybe it's a career choice in a certain field, or you could need an unusual name, or even a nickname, or perhaps it's a type of weapon you would like to use in a scene. We touch on a number of areas for quick ideas to get you going.

What is *Writer's Secret Weapon?*

It's an idea sparker, a way to add to your story. With this book, you'll not only learn great tips for writers, but you will also find lists of quick ideas for story components that will keep you going at any point during the writing process—in the middle of writing your novel, just starting your outline, putting together your character biographies, trying to meet a deadline, or stuck with writer's block. Wherever you find yourself, *WSW* can help.

Writer's Secret Weapon is for all fiction writers. We all know how to Google, but many times we don't know where to start to get to that idea. This guide can save you hours of searching and going down rabbit holes when you should be writing instead. We wrote a book we would have liked to have earlier in our own careers, and to use now. We believe this guide will spur you on in your writing career.

About the authors:

Cheyenne McCray fell in love with reading and writing early, deciding in kindergarten that one day she would become an author. Today, she is an award-winning *New York Times* and *USA Today* bestselling fiction author who's sold millions of print and electronic, traditionally and indie published books worldwide. Having published more than 100 novels and novellas in contemporary and paranormal romance, urban fantasy and romantic suspense, she is currently kicking off a new chapter in her career, writing cozy mysteries as Deb Ries.

During her 20-year career, Chey has read an enormous amount, gone to and given countless workshops, been on numerous panels, taken many classes, and attended multiple conferences. She believes you can walk away from any form of education having learned something new. Whatever your skill level, you might try out a new idea and find it takes your career to a new level. Chey has mentored numerous authors and believes in paying it forward. She hopes you will find ideas here that spark your imagination and let it fly!

After working in the corporate world as an accountant, H.D. Thomson changed her focus to one of her passions—books. She owned and operated an online bookstore for several years, and now writes romantic suspense, paranormal, and contemporary romance featuring tortured heroes and ordinary people in extraordinary circumstances. She has spent years learning the craft, experiencing and adapting to mammoth changes in the writing industry, and her books have won and finaled in numerous competitions, including the RWA's Golden Heart, Suzannah, and Emily contests.

She also owns and operates Bella Media Management, which specializes in websites, video trailers, eBook conversion, and promotional resources for authors and small businesses. Having focused on numerous tools and techniques to get a book published, she's spoken at workshops on covers, formatting, social media, and the general writing industry. H.D. loves working with writers and knows she can help fellow authors, new or experienced, navigate the various mine fields in publishing.

From the authors:

We believe you will find *Writer's Secret Weapon* useful to get you over a hurdle, break through a mental barrier, or trigger your creativity. If you have any questions or feedback, or think of anything you'd like to see included in the next edition, feel free to email us at BellaMediaManagement@gmail.com.

Thanks for joining the *Writer's Secret Weapon* family, and enjoy the ride in your own writing career!

Cheyenne and H.D.

IMAGERY

When a reader is swept up in a novel and is so engrossed in the story that they forget their surroundings, imagery is involved. There are seven types of imagery: visual (sight), olfactory (smell), gustatory (taste), tactile (touch), auditory (hearing), kinesthetic (feeling of movement), and organic (feeling through actions).

Imagery is powerful. Be specific and vivid, and include all the senses when feasible. Help your readers create the scene in their own mind. Look back at those times you've tried to describe a scene to someone else—it's more than action, more than a picture. The scene has multiple layers.

Organic imagery is probably the hardest to explain. Through the character's actions, the writer reveals what this person is feeling. When your heroine is exhausted, imagery can be conveyed by her sliding deeper into the sofa, bowing her head, or rubbing at her brow.

Smell is tied to olfactory imagery. This is where the author conveys scent in a scene. Pungent examples are gardenias, garlic, and gasoline. In H.D.'s novel, *Identity*, she uses olfactory imagery. Scent is probably the most powerful imagery to connect to the memories and the past.

As Skye washed her hands, the scent of the woman's toothpaste assailed her senses.

Peppermint.

The smell drove a wave of anxiety through her body. Peppermint. That smell. She hated it, couldn't rid herself of the odor as it clung to her nose. She forced air in and out of her lungs.

A picture flared in her mind's eye. Her hands gripped the arms of a chair from her past. Metal clamps kept her wrists tied to the leather. A person stood to her right and along her peripheral vision.

Kinesthetic imagery involves movement and is used in poetry to create actions. It can either be through an object or character. Words and action are tied together. A simple example is when you have your character twirl on the lawn and moonlight illuminates the blades of grass beneath her bare feet.

In *Hidden Prey* from Cheyenne McCray, she uses tactile and kinesthetic in the following example:

Tori groaned, her mind spinning with pain and confusion. She felt dizzy and unable to form a coherent thought.

Her whole body ached and stung and it hurt to breathe. She tried to raise her head, but pain lanced her skull and she clasped her head with her hands.

Tori lay on something hard and cold, the chill seeping through her body. She shivered and her eyes watered as yet another stabbing pain went through her chest.

She opened her eyelids and blinked until her eyes adjusted to the dimness. She lay on a concrete floor and bars filled her vision. Another shiver went through her as she realized someone had put her into a cell.

Below are imagery lists broken into the seven categories. Hopefully, they'll be a springboard to something exciting.

Feel free to use any of these examples that you might find useful in your own writing!

OLFACTORY IMAGERY

She breathed in the tang of the sea
Nothing smelled better than coffee in the morning
The fragrance of roses lingered in the air
The odor of mildew and sweaty socks made her want to hold her breath
Bile rose in her throat as the stench of death escaped the room
He smelled of sun-warmed skin and testosterone
A bouquet of scents met her when she walked into the orchid hothouse
Sugary treats sweetened the air and drew them into the bakery
The burning sandalwood incense relaxed her
The smell of the old man's cherry pipe tobacco reminded her of her father
Jasmine perfume conjured up memories of her trip to Asia
Marijuana smoke floated through the room and filled his nostrils
The big jar of pickles and its briny smell carried him back to younger days
She kicked leaves across the lawn, enjoying the crisp scent of fall
The lingering odor of cigarettes told him someone had been there
The strong smell of printer ink made her lightheaded
Warm, balmy nights in the tropics carried scents of rum and pineapple
The wine's bouquet carried complex notes of tart cherries and dark chocolate
The garbage and rotting food stench nearly made him vomit
He hated the antiseptic smells of hospitals
The smell of freshly baked bread made its way out of the kitchen
Men seemed to follow the intoxicating scent of her floral perfume
Billows of black smoke accompanied the stench of burning rubber
The clean scent of rain-washed skies followed the storm
Her lip gloss smelled like bubblegum
The pungent aroma of garlic emanated from the kitchen
The odors of greasy hamburgers and fries caused her stomach to churn
Smells of freshly mown grass took her back to her childhood
The sharp aroma of peppermint cleared her sinuses

She always smelled like the fruity gum she chewed
He smelled like sour beer and stale cigarettes
A stink like rotten meat clogged her nose
A whiff of orange blossom-scented air trailed after her
The scent of sandalwood reminded her of old times with her father
The herb garden smelled of mint and rosemary
The kids sniffed markers in the classroom to get high
The tanning lotion's coconut scent made her think of days at the pool
He gagged at the rotten egg odor
The scent of his spicy aftershave teased her senses
She loved libraries and the musty scent of old books
The stench of the decomposing body caused her to vomit

AUDITORY IMAGERY

The dog's incessant barking made him grit his teeth

The rapping of knuckles on the door startled her out of her daydream

She shouted down the well and her words echoed back to her

Blaring horns and growls of revving engines filled the street

Wind rushing through the trees reminded her of the sound of the sea

The pounding of his heart thrummed in his ears

The refrigerator hum seemed loud in the empty house

A creak of an opening door made her heart pound

Ocean waves crashed to the shore like cymbals in a marching band

The baby's squall told her that he was ill

The owl's screech raked her spine

Her raspy voice made it difficult to understand what she said

Wind howled through cracks in the boards

She rested her head on his chest and heard his heartbeat against her ear

The house groaned from aftershocks of the earthquake

Branches scraped across the side of the barn

The cat yowled its anger

Chalk squeaked across the chalkboard

The little girl's squeal expressed her delight

A burst of static issued from the old radio

The pen scratched across the paper

His shout startled the boy

The screen door banged open

The mattress springs creaked

The snake's rattle caused him to stiffen

Water gurgled down the drain

The babbling brook sounded like fairy laughter

An alarm clock buzzed in another room

The sonic boom disrupted the formerly quiet afternoon

The old woman's cackle set her on edge
Chatter and laughter came from the cafeteria
The wooden train clacked over its rails
A bell's clang indicated the start of a religious service
His ankle chains clanked as he shuffled between the guards
The audience's clapping thundered throughout the room
He clattered down the stairs
Coins clinked together as they tumbled through the machine
The explosion deafened him
She hummed a lullaby to the sleeping child
The constant jabber made it difficult to concentrate
The creak of the antique rocking chair cut through the silence

GUSTATORY IMAGERY

He tasted salt on her skin
The flavor of crisp red apples reminded him of fall days
He enjoyed the beer's bitter taste of hops
The milk chocolate melted on her tongue
The icing tasted so sweet it hurt her teeth
She savored every bite of the pistachio ice cream
The hot sauce had a real kick to it and her mouth felt on fire
He found malt vinegar less acidic than apple cider vinegar
Dark chocolate's bittersweet flavor is her favorite
The sour candy made her mouth pucker
The dish was too briny for her palate
She almost vomited when she drank the sour milk
The dessert's bright, citrusy flavor made her think of being in the tropics
The cooling flavor of mint added a nice touch to the meal
He enjoyed an earthy red wine
Fiery habanero peppers burned her tongue
The vegetables tasted light and crisp
The herbal remedy tasted vile
Cream-filled pastries had the richest flavor
She ate the honeyed fruit with pleasure
The rich, full-bodied wine felt heavy in her mouth
The best cheeses had a nutty flavor in her opinion
Port has a robust taste
Sharp cheeses have the strongest flavor
He liked the smoky barbeque sauce the best
The tang of citrus tingled in his mouth
Tart cherries made it a not-so-sweet dessert
The bread tasted both yeasty and salty
The coffee had a woody, earthy edge to it

Zesty key lime pie resided on the menu
Fresh pomegranate has an astringent flavor
The fish had a brackish taste
The savory quiche had a strong garlic flavor
She had never like syrupy desserts
Unsalted pork tastes bland
Watery porridge is unappealing
Tasty sweet and sour chicken is his favorite Chinese food
The well-seasoned beef rounded out the meal
Ripe peaches are the sweetest fruit
The mild chili had no bite to it

TACTILE IMAGERY

Soft grass tickled her bare feet
Goose bumps pebbled her skin
The welcome chill of ice helped alleviate pain from the burn
She giggled as fish nibbled at her toes
His callused fingertips felt as rough as a cat's tongue
She felt hot and sticky beneath her clothing in the humid night
The bottle felt cool to his touch
Whiskey burned his throat and warmed his belly
His stubble abraded her skin like sandpaper
Every strike of his shoe against earth reverberated through him as he ran
Flying debris stung her cheeks
She rubbed her damp palms over the soft fabric of her slacks
Her skin felt like leather
She stroked his fur that was like silk to her touch
He tumbled, snow stinging his face and rocks jabbing his skin
The cold chilled her through
The dust-covered end table felt gritty to his touch
Branches scratched her bare legs
His skin felt stretched taut
His rough grip bruised her flesh
The horse's velvety muzzle brushed his palm.
Her eyes stung with tears
She screamed from the burning pain as he poured salt onto the gash
The popped blister on the back of her heel stung
Warm blood seeped from his body and over her hand
The hot cereal burned her tongue
Her head ached like someone had driven an ice pick through her eye
The metal file abraded her skin
The needle pricked his finger

He tickled her with a downy feather
Clothing hung in a soggy mess from her body
Phantom pains made him feel like his missing fingers tingled
She dug her fingernails into her palms
He ground his teeth
Her knuckles ached from slamming her fist into his jaw
Warm, sticky snot rolled onto his upper lip
Her sunburn was hot to the touch
Pain shot through his broken limb like a lance
He skidded across the asphalt, shredding his flesh
Rose thorns scratched her arm

KINESTHETIC IMAGERY

She skipped across the lawn
He snatched his hand back when the pot handle's heat seared his palm
She dipped her feet into the still pond
He gripped her wrist
The sea breeze moistened the air
He slammed a mallet on her head, dropping her
He jogged along the path that wound through the pines
The windstorm slapped her face
Hair rose at her nape
Sweat slid down his spine
He nuzzled the curve of her neck
The dog pushed his muzzle under her hand
She skimmed her fingertips through the water
He slid his palm along the banister
She bolted through the jungle
The man grabbed her around her waist
The mare snuffled against the boy's open hand
Blood covered her hands as she tried to stem the flow
The dog clamped his jaws on the man's leg
A tear rolled down her cheek in a hot trail
An apple dropped from the tree
He pushed the needle through the fabric
The auctioneer chanted rapid-fire
His bones ached in the winter
The little girl skipped along
The kids played hopscotch
She scrabbled up the mountainside
He sneezed and his throat ached
He blazed a trail through life

The cat yowled its anger
She sneezed into a tissue
He rubbed the substance into her wound
The corners of her eyes crinkled when she laughed
The bird trilled and burst into song
Her hair floated around her shoulders in the breeze
She walked on clouds
The condor flapped its great wings
Her hips swayed as she sauntered over to him
He slung his backpack over his shoulder
She tossed the garbage into the dumpster
The dog bared its teeth and growled
The thought popped into her mind
Her face grew hot

ORGANIC IMAGERY

EXCITED/HAPPY

She bounced up and down on her toes
A grin split his face
She danced around the room
He jumped and mimed sinking a basketball in a hoop and scoring
She clapped and jumped to her feet
He pumped his fist
She was at a loss for words
He gave a thumbs up
He pretended to give a celebratory dance in the endzone
She hummed a catchy tune
He sang along with the radio
She skipped across the yard
He hugged her to him
She flung out her arms and spun in circles.
He picked up his pace, wanting to get there faster
Her lips curved into a grin
He threw his head back and laughed
She straightened her shoulders and raised her head
She dissolved into fits of giggles
She squealed and jumped up and down

SURPRISE/SHOCK

His eyes widened
She clapped her hand over her mouth
His chin dropped and his mouth fell open
She gasped as she stared at him

She put her hand to her heart
He yelped and spun around
She froze, rooted to the spot
He raised his hands into the air
He gripped the back of the chair to keep from falling
She stared in astonishment
He felt speechless
Her heart skipped a beat
She couldn't breathe
She clasped her hands to her chest
He stumbled back, unable to believe it
Her skin tingled and hair rose at her nape
Her breath caught in her throat
Her heart beat so hard her chest ached
Her knees gave out on her and she collapsed to the floor
He tried to remember how to breathe

DEJECTION/SADDNESS/DISAPPOINTMENT

He slumped on the couch
A feeling of dread grew in his chest
She hung her head
A tear rolled down her cheek
Her lower lip trembled
He swallowed and turned away
She stared at the ground as she walked
He felt numb
She put her hand to her throat
She held the pillow tight to her chest
He dragged his feet
He felt as if a lead weight weighed down his gut
She felt dizzy, unable to focus
She spoke in a low tone, her words shaky
Her heart sank

His skin grew cold
He focused on a spot on the wall and struggled to rein in his emotions
He buried his face in his palms
Voices faded around her
Her eyes ached with unshed tears

EMBARASSMENT/SHAME

His face flushed and heat burned his cheeks
She slid down in her seat, trying not to be seen
She covered her face with her hands
She wished the floor would open up and swallow her whole
He coughed and avoided her gaze
Her lower lip trembled
He stared at his feet
She tried to change the subject
Her skin felt clammy
He wanted to bury his head in the sand like an ostrich
He stared away into nothing
She pulled at a loose thread on her sleeve
He banged his head against the wall
He did a face-palm, unable to believe what he'd just done
He fidgeted with a button on his shirt
Heat flooded her as she felt all eyes on her
He steppcd away from her, his face hot
She bit her lower lip
His shoulders drooped
She rubbed her sweaty palms on her jeans

ANGER

He narrowed his gaze
She stomped up to him
He ground his teeth

She balled her hands into fists
He flung a chair across the room
He stalked away from her
Her spine went rigid and her muscles stiffened
Her skin burned
He bit back a curse
Her scalp tingled
She felt the seconds tick away as he scowled at her
Fury boiled up inside her
He jabbed his finger into his friend's chest
She stared up at the ceiling and counted to ten
He clenched his jaw
She folded her arms and glared
He clenched his hands into fists
Heat blazed inside him
He slammed his fist into the wall
A vein in his forehead throbbed

PAIN

The pain burned inside her as if a poisoned arrow had punctured her belly
Her chest felt like she was being eaten from the inside out
His lungs burned as he struggled to breathe
Searing pain radiated to every part of her body
He felt as if someone had driven a sword through his gut
Electric shocks shot down her spine
The gash on her thigh felt like it had been ripped open by a shredder
A dull throb ached behind his eye
Her chest felt as if a boulder crushed her
The sharp, localized pain made her feel like someone had driven a stake into her thigh
The wound pulsated with fire
Every movement sent bursts of pain through his body
Pain pounded in her head like a jackhammer

Her ankle screamed in pain

His gut felt like a rusty dagger had ripped him in two

Shock waves of pain pulsed through her chest

He felt like fire ants were biting him on every inch of skin

He gritted his teeth, holding back a cry

A sob rose inside her and she blinked away tears as she tried not to focus on the pain

Her head felt like it had split open

FATIGUE

The mere thought of movement exhausted her

She fumbled with her pen, then pushed it away, too tired to write

Even coffee with double shots of espresso couldn't keep her awake

Her bones felt like concrete

He could barely put one foot in front of the other

Her muscles groaned

He felt lethargic, not interested in anything but sleep

Words wouldn't come easily to him

Nothing seemed to make sense

Her eyes blurred from the need to sleep

She had zero energy to do more than sip her coffee

She couldn't keep her eyes open

Her puffy eyelids made it difficult to blink

He slumped on the couch and felt like he might sink into it

He forced himself to concentrate on one thing at a time to get through the day

She felt like she had to hold onto something to keep from crumpling to the ground

She felt listless, not really caring about anything

He couldn't seem to remember the simplest things

She kept hoping for a second wind, but it never came

He couldn't think clearly

THIRST/HUNGER

She swayed, lightheaded from it being too long since her last meal
His throat ached for something to drink
She licked her parched lips
Her dry mouth tasted like sand
A gnawing pain ached in his empty belly
She grew weak from dehydration
He salivated at the thought of food
Hunger gnawed at his belly
He could eat a rhinoceros whole
The burning sensation in his belly increased the longer it had been since his last meal
Her blood sugar dipped and she trembled
He'd gone too long since his last meal and by this point he was beyond hungry
He had grown irritable, and he stumbled on shaky legs
She could drink Lake Erie and not quench her thirst
He felt hollow inside, as if he could never eat enough
His energy level dropped and he couldn't focus
The smell of roast beef made his mouth water
She craved deep dish pizza
He had gone so long without a decent meal, his ribs protruded
She'd stab his hand with a fork if he tried to start without her

VISUAL IMAGERY

Moonlight played across her features, a silvery lover caressing soft skin.

The hills rose in a sweep of green, a majestic backdrop to homes marred by weed-choked yards, sagging porches, and broken windows.

The insect of a car bounced over the pothole-riddled street.

The ash tree had lost all but one brown leaf, which waved in the breeze as if saying goodbye before it would fall free of its branch and float down to join its brothers and sisters.

She braced her hand on the worn shovel handle as she looked down at her handiwork, then frowned when she saw a pale thumb sticking from the mound.

He played the video game with ferocity, the controller vibrating in his hands as he punched buttons and thrust the toggle from side to side.

The curtains parted and a moon-like face peered through the gap.

Condensation rolled down the sides of the brown beer bottle as he scraped at the label with his thumbnail.

Shadow's sides heaved in her sleep, the dog's paws jerking as though chasing rabbits in farmer Rick's potato field.

Perspiration trailed along his spine as he clenched the bouquet of pink roses tightly in one fist while pressing the brass doorbell with his other hand.

The petite girl gripped the racecar in her small hand as she pushed the toy along the curve of the racetrack.

His athletic shoes pounded hard earth, his breathing labored as he pushed himself to run faster up the leaf-strewn hill.

Grass bent beneath the girl's boots as she kicked at cow patties while walking across the pasture.

The Appaloosa raised her head from the feed trough as her spotted hide shivered to chase away buzzing flies.

Children giggled as they chased each other around squat picnic tables laden with barbeque ribs and potato salad.

Dust motes danced in the shaft of sunlight that tumbled through the living room window to the brown shag carpet below.

The father tucked his curly-headed child into bed, drawing the cozy comforter up to the girl's chin before he settled on the rocking chair to tell stories of princesses and fairies in faraway lands.

Orange and yellow fall leaves scattered in plumes as the girl bolted across the neighbor's yard, a golden retriever bounding in her wake.

Rust rimmed the ancient refrigerator's doors, its hum sounding like an old man's rasping cough.

Her heels echoed a sharp staccato on marble tile as she entered the expansive foyer and she slammed down her purse with a thud on the carved table near the door.

The patina on the surface of the antique violin shone in the soft glow emanating from the track lighting.

She stared at the corpse, the skin like moldy cottage cheese, and she fought to keep from vomiting on the detective's shoes.

She whistled while washing the crystal, each wine glass sparkling in the sunshine pouring through the kitchen window.

A double rainbow crossed the rain-washed sky, and she imagined at each end leprechauns with four-leaf clovers in their hats sat on fat pots of gold.

The man's shoulders hunched as he used his pointer fingers to punch the antique typewriter's keys in painful and deliberate movements.

Sunlight sparkled on the bay as she shielded her eyes with her hand and watched the fisherman's weathered boat make its way into the harbor.

The heavens glittered as they lay on their backs on the old wedding ring quilt and wished on shooting stars.

She had etched every detail on the pottery with great care before smashing the bowl onto the floor and scattering fragments across the room.

He kicked dirt clods and rocks as he walked, stirring up dust to coat his formerly shiny black church shoes, just to tick off that woman who called herself Auntie.

She hummed as she cultivated lavender, nasturtiums, and strawberries around tiny pieces of furniture provided for fairies to rest and enjoy their nectar in teacups made from rose petals.

The sound of lawn sprinklers and cicadas made her sleepy as she rocked in the hammock tied between the pair of old willow trees.

He tapped his pencil eraser on the lined college-ruled paper, trying to think of something, anything, to write that would make his teacher sit up and take notice and know he wasn't a stupid boy.

The calico walked across the laptop's keyboard, spelling strange words with her steps, as if offering a coded message that would explain every thought she wanted to express.

She walked through the curtain of beads into a room spotted with lava lamps, and walls covered by neon posters that glowed in the black light.

He drove his dagger into her chest and twisted it as she screamed. Blood poured from the wound, staining the white blouse red.

The wind lifted her hair from her shoulders, the strands gleaming strawberry-blonde in the early morning light.

She tugged the too-short skirt as far as she could down her thighs, praying the fabric wouldn't slide up and reveal her lacy panties.

The sudden absence of bird song caused her to still mid-step, her shoe hovering over pine needles before a twig snapped behind her.

He smashed his fist into the wall, chunks of drywall dropping onto the floor and chalk-white covering his hand as he ground his teeth pulled it out of the new hole.

The waterfall pounded into the pool, and he glanced through the curtain of water to see glimpses of the fiery demon on the other side.

SETTINGS, WRITING PROMPTS & ACTIVITIES

Where to place the next event in your story? Settings can inspire you to create more vivid and interesting scenes. Sometimes you wrack your brain, trying to come up with something new. There are thousands of possibilities, yet often we get stuck on the same few settings. This guide offers over 300 ideas for settings, many of which may be different than anything you've tried before.

Having a hard time coming up with an interesting, fun, or even a sucky day out or a date night for your characters? Inside *WSW*, you'll find more than 250 different possibilities for where your characters might hang out, enjoy themselves, or have a totally rotten time. You're bound to discover something that inspires you and your characters.

Within the following pages, you'll find lists of hobbies for your characters, charities they might work with, the arts they might enjoy, and sports to participate in, along with a list of toys and games for adults and kids.

We have also included 300 prompts to stimulate ideas for your story. These are quick one-line ideas to help trigger thoughts for your novel. One prompt might even inspire a new book. Skim through the lists and see what you come up with!

SCENE SETTINGS

Looking for a certain mood in your scene? Enjoy writing dialogue but now you've got to add some type of location to your work of art? We've found over 300 settings that will make you wonder, "Wow, why didn't I think of that?"

Adoption clinic
Airplane
Ambulance
Amphitheater
Amusement park
Antique store
Arch
Art gallery
Attic
Badlands
Bakery
Balcony
Bank
Bar
Barbershop
Barn dance
Basketball court
Bath
Bath house
Beach
Beaver dam
Bird's nest
Birthday party
Black sand beach
Blacksmith

Blimp
Blowhole
Boat
Boot camp
Border
Breakfast nook
Brewery
Bridge
Butterfly habitat
Café
Cage
Camping
Campsite
Canyon
Cape
Car
Castle
Cat lady's house
Cathedral
Causeway
Cave
Cavern
Cemetery
Charity auction
Cheese factory

Chessboard
Chiropractor's office
Church
Circus
Cliff diving
Cliffs
Coast
Coffee shop
Column
Corral
Country
County or state fair
Court
Crater
Crater lake
Creek
Criminal hideout
Cruise ship
Dance studio
Deep sea diving
Deli
Department of Motor Vehicles
Desert
Detention
Diner
Dinner table
Dollar store
Drunk tank
Easter bunny at the mall
Elephant sanctuary
Elevator
Emergency room
Execution chamber
Exhibit

Falls
Farm
Farmer's market
Fault line
Ferris wheel
Finish line
Fire station
Fishing boat
Five-star dining
Flat tire
Flatland
Fondue restaurant
Flower garden
Football field
Forest
Fortune teller's shop
Fossil hunting grounds
Fountain
Garage
Garbage dump
Garden
Gate
Ghost town
Glade
Gold mine
Golf course
Gondola
Grocery store
Grotto
Gulch
Gulf
Gypsy camp
Hair salon
Hardware store

Haunted house	Lake
Health resort	Landmark
Helicopter	Laundromat
Henhouse	Lava flow
Hiking trails	Lava-covered lands
Hockey rink	Library
Holiday dinner table	Lifeboat
Holiday party	Lighthouse
Hollowed-out stone	Lunchroom
Honeycomb caves	Make-up counter
Horse stable	Marsh
Hospital	Mechanic's shop
Hospital room	Mine
Hunting trip	Mom and pop restaurant
Hut	Mosque
Ice cream shop	Mountain
Ice shelf	Mountain rim
Ice-covered country	Mummy's tomb
Ice-filled cave	Museum
Iceberg	Named landmarks
Igloo	Nature trail
Island	News station
Japanese garden	Nightclub
Jet pilot cockpit	Nude beach
Jewelry store	Nursing home
Judge's chambers	Oasis
Jungle	Ocean
Jury box	Office
Karaoke bar	Office cubicle
Karate class	Open house—real estate
Kitchen sink	Optometrist
Knitting circle	Orchard
Lagoon	Orchestra pit
Lair	Overpass

Palace
Pantheon
Park
Peak
Pet store
Petrified forest
Petroglyphs
Photography class
Picnic
Pirate ship
Pit
Plains
Police station
Pond
Post office
Principal's office
Prom
Pub
Pyramid
Quilting circle
Quiz show
Radio program
Rainforest
Ranch
Red carpet
Redwood forest
Reef
Region
Repair shop
Restaurant
Restaurant grand opening
Retail stores
Reunion
Ridge

River
Riverboat
Road trips
Roadside
Rock forest
Rock formations
Rock garden
Roller coaster
Rooftop dining
Rose garden
Rotating restaurant
Ruins
Safari
Salt mine
Saltwater river
Sand dune
Santa at the mall
Santa's lap
Santa's workshop
Scenic lookout
School lunchroom
School nurse's office
Schoolroom
Sea
Secondhand store
Ship
Sink hole
Skate park
Ski jump
Ski slope
Ski tram
Sky train
Sky tram
Snow-covered country

Social club
Softball game
Spider web
Spring
Stadium
Submarine
Subterranean lake
Subway
Summer camp
Survival camp
Swamp
Temple
Thrift store
Tourist trap
Tower
Trade show
Train
Training grounds
Travel agency
Treehouse
Tribal ceremony
Truckstop
Tunnel
Underground
Underwater

Unemployment office
Valley
Vatican
Village
Volcano—dead
Volcano—live
Volleyball court
Voting booth
Wall
Warehouse
Water park
Waterfall
Wedding
White House
Wild West tourist town
Wildlife preserve
Woodshop class
Wrestling ring
X-ray lab
Yard sale
Yacht
Yearbook club
Yoga class
Zoo

WRITING PROMPTS

Don't know where to go next? Having a bad case of writer's block and don't see it ending soon? Here are 300 prompts to jump-start your creative ideas. We dare you to try one.

PEOPLE

Businessman finds a body in the park
Couple goes to Thailand and finds ivory elephant
Elderly man goes scuba diving with swimsuit model
Elderly man raises orchids
Elderly woman finds a pendant she lost as a girl
Elderly woman finds twin she never knew she had
Grandfather goes ice skating
Grandfather goes on hike with son and grandson
Grandfather loses lucky penny he's had since childhood
Grandfather wears local college team's mascot uniform
Grandmother beats grandchildren at video games
Grandmother finds an old charm
Grandmother loses dentures
Grandmother reads Dr. Scuss book to grandchildren
Mail carrier trips over dead body
Man builds bomb, blows up his car collection
Man changes careers from business to ranching
Man eats chocolate-covered crickets
Man gets braces in his fifties
Man loses his mind teaching junior high students
Man picks up hitchhiking twins
Man sets fire to women's underwear
Man starts gum wrapper collection

Man takes up playing fiddle in his sixties
Man teaches art to high school students
Man visits old friend in hospice
Mime plays hopscotch with kids
Motorcycle gang member runs over pizza
Nun flies a kite
Priest finds a rubber ducky in the confessional
Professional bowler goes bowling with senior citizen team
Scientist finds a dead person in her lab
Sous chef drops bottle of chili into soup
Three grandmothers play Pokémon Go
Two old friends play on swings in a park
Violinist is attacked with her own bow
Woman accidentally turns her hair bright green
Woman backpacks alone through Europe
Woman stops to pick up hitchhiker
Woman finds an old, dirty teddy bear
Woman finds sister's toy from when she was a child
Woman goes back to school for a master's degree
Woman goes sky diving in Cabo
Woman joins Red Hat ladies for high tea
Woman makes memory quilt with daughter
Woman plays bingo with a stranger, who wins
Woman pulls up floorboards and finds treasure
Woman rescues man from burning car
Woman wins marathon then drops dead at finish line

CHILDREN & YOUNG ADULTS

Baby breaks grandmother's pearl necklace
Baby grabs man's beard
Baby spits up on back of man's neck in movie theatre
Baby's diaper stinks up courtroom
Boy brings home an injured duck

Boy climbs a food display
Boy fills toilet with pebbles and toy cars
Boy puts shaving cream on guest while sleeping
Boy steps on man's glasses in a park
Boy wakes up baby sister to make her cry
Boy wins international art contest
Child finds parents' handgun in cedar chest
Child found by police officer in her cruiser
Child genius speaks five languages
Child gets lost in the mall
Child makes balloon animal for a clown
Child prodigy acts out all of Shakespeare's plays
Child runs away from home and hides in candy store
Firefighter rescues pet rabbit for little girl
Girl breaks her arm on the playground
Girl finds homeless child in a hidden room
Girl kicks butt at playing HORSE
Girl publishes her first book at ten-years-old
Girl puts frog in man's breakfast cereal
Girl turns mom's purse into flower garden
Girl wins skateboard competition
Kids collect dimes for the homeless and raise $1 million
Kids compete in video game contest
Kids jump bikes on riverbank
Kids play hide and seek in the attic
Kids set fire to county courthouse
Kids shoplift Troll dolls
Kids start dog rescue shelter
Teen gets a strange fortune in a cookie
Teen gets invited to the presidential inauguration
Teen plays tuba in high school marching band
Teen rescues malnourished cat
Teen rollerblades a hundred miles
Teen trains Arabian horses

Teen visits elderly patients in long-term care facility
Teen wins Pulitzer Prize for peace
Teen wins trip to Washington D.C.
Teen works at runaway shelter
Teens get even with principal and teachers in dunking booth
Toddler breaks Ming vase
Toddler eats bug collection
Toddler falls into lake and is saved by teen
Toddler wakes up a guest by banging pots by his head
Toddler walks three miles from home

TRAVEL/TRANSPORTATION

Aircraft carrier hits tanker and splits in two
Airplane lands on country road
ATV quad flips on top of buried house
Bike rider falls into cement
Boat hits alligator
Bus load of retirees go to Vegas
Canoe springs a leak in middle of the lake
Car crashes into a house
Cruise ship hits a sandbar
Dump truck breaks down on one-lane bridge
Gondola capsizes in waterway
Harrier jet crashes in cornfield
Helicopter rotor snaps off
Helicopter snags power line
Hot air balloon catches fire at festival
Hovercraft crashes into museum
Jet pack explodes in air
Jet ski runs out of gas a mile from shore
Motorbike gets flat tire in front of biker bar
Motorboat runs up onto island shore
Motorcycle breaks down on a lonely dirt road

Motorhome slides off side of mountain
Parachute snags on cliff
Parasail event cancelled on account of murder
Pedicab driver spills passengers into river
Person has a heart attack on moped
Rickshaw's tire comes off
Rowboat's remaining oar breaks
Sailboat gets lost at sea
Semi-truck crashes and spills a load of milk
Small airplane crashes into mountain
Snowmobile runs out of gas five miles from home
Speedboat gets snagged in lobster trap lines
Stealth jet lands on high school campus
Stealth ship/hydrofoil lands with Marines
Submarine caught by giant squid
Subway train jumps off the rails
Tank levels house by mistake
Tractor holds up traffic
Train derails after hitting car on tracks
Train runs over a penny
Tram falls into ten feet of snow
Travel trailer comes unhitched on mountain road
Truck breaks down on freeway
Truck runs off mountain into top floor of house
Tugboat catches on fire
Vintage car crashes into candy store
Yacht sinks with a casket filled with gold

NATURE

Asteroid turns forest into a crater
Avalanche buries ski resort
Bird droppings land on picnic food
Blizzard dumps 100 inches of snow on small town

Cave collapses with teenagers inside
Cold wave wipes out farm crops
Comet burns up over small country and destroys it
Drought devastates water supplies
Earthquake destroys a car dealership
Electrical storm destroys cell phone towers
Fault line swallows forest
Flood destroys theme park
Hailstorm the size of golf balls damages Porsche
Heat wave causes cars to catch on fire
Hurricane destroys a theme park
Ice cracks and collapses while boy walks across a lake
Ice storm downs power lines
Landslide fills small lake
Large hailstorm shatters glass factory
Lava flow slowly eats up small neighborhood
Lightning strikes a church
Lightning strikes the bedroom
Meteor shower pummels island
Monsoon wipes out a farm
Moonlight illuminates strange object on shore
Mudslide takes out chocolate factory
Rain washes out bridge
River overflows onto farmlands
Sandstorm fills swimming pools
Sinkhole swallows up a lawyer's office
Snow causes roof to collapse
Solar flare disrupts power grid
Sun bakes cookies on dashboard
Sun fries egg on sidewalk
Thunderstorm scares large man to tears
Tidal wave destroys eccentric man's private city
Tornado takes out the town's only bar
Tree limb crashes onto a barbecue

Tree spontaneously bursts into flames
Tsunami wipes out nuclear reactor
Typhoon destroys tourist resort
Volcanic ash buries large farm
Volcano eruption destroys small town
Waterfall hides an old shipwreck
Wildfire takes out ice cream factory
Wind blows weathervane into car
Windstorm blows away windmill
Winter storm hits popsicle factory

ANIMALS/INSECTS

Angry bull chases man in a pasture
Bats swarm out of cave
Beehive falls to the ground
Bee lands on a popsicle
Bird flies into the house
Bird makes nest in WWII helmet
Black widow spider bites man in garage
Camel wanders by the freeway in winter
Cat coughs up a hairball
Cat kills family gerbil
Cat sneaks up on pet tortoise
Cockroach in the bathtub
Come across a hibernaculum of snakes inside a cave
Cows break out of slaughterhouse and stampede
Dog chases a skunk into the yard
Dog defecates in neighbor's yard
Dog eats a sock
Dog gets thorn in paw
Dog licks rabbit's face
Dog pack chases a rabbit
Dog steals a rag doll

Duck wears a costume
Elephant paints picture with its trunk
Flea infestation spreads rare disease
Gophers dig up golf course
Gorillas break out of zoo
Howling coyotes go silent
Hummingbirds swarm flower garden
Iguana gets loose in a classroom
Ladybug lands in a glass of soda
Lizard scares a man
Monkey eats rat poison
Parrot bites cat in butt
Plague of grasshoppers eat every leaf in neighborhood
Poisonous snake is mistaken for a garter snake
Police dog takes down rapist
Puppy wanders into elementary school
Scorpion stings woman in dark closet
Skunk walks into a biker bar
Snake crawls into running shoe
Snake starts rattling feet away
Spider appears from under a pillow
Spider builds web in a knitting bag
Squirrel steals marbles
Termites eat through beams supporting living room floor
Toddler puts cat into goldfish bowl
Truck crashes and cows escape onto the freeway
Wild boar chases a man

DISASTERS

Air tank malfunction while a diver is deep underwater
Airplane goes down with over a hundred passengers
Bridge collapses on engineers
Bus goes off side of mountain

Cable car plows into department store
Church bell falls from tower
Church piano falls through floor
Coaster loses control during race down mountain streets
Copper mine collapses below ground
Crane falls off of building and kills protesters
Cruise ship's engines fail in the middle of the ocean
Dam breaks, floods lake, and overflows
Drilling accident kills workers and causes underwater oil spill
Electrical fire in barn
Explosion at a nuclear plant happens near city
Famine kills thousands
Fire consumes historic courthouse in small town
Fire in fireworks warehouse
Fire melts chocolate in factory
Flu epidemic wipes out small town
Food contamination in beef processing plant
Frying pan catches fire
Gas leak causes mass evacuation
Groundwater is contaminated from a factory
Herbicide killing farmers in the area
Historic cannon blows up at Fourth of July celebration
Hot air balloon catches on fire
Hundreds get a gastrointestinal illness on a cruise ship
Ice cream store catches fire
Kids find a basement when the town's tornado alert goes off
Marble factory explodes, rains marble hail
Milk tanker truck spill results in sour milk smell downtown
Oil spill hitting the coast
Radiation leaking into the water
Radio station blows a fuse
Rioting over unfair ruling by judge
Robbers hold hostages in bank
Rocks break sailboat hull

Roller coaster jumps rails at amusement park
Roof caves in on firework store
Ski tram plunges onto slope
Static charge at gas pumps blows up convenience store
Stock market crashes after person transfers to risky funds
Survivalists plant bombs in law enforcement office
Terrorists poison water supply
Trapped on the freeway while a hurricane/tornado strikes
Tree hits the roof where a baby sleeps
Yacht runs into rocks near lighthouse

ACTIVITIES

THE ARTS

Need a character with a talent in the arts or looking to perform in an orchestra? We have numerous ideas to help!

ARTS

Actor
Architecture
Art showing
Ballet
Ceramics
Cinema/motion picture
Cinematography
Comedian/stand-up
Dance
Drama
Drawing
Literature
Music

Opera
Orchestra/Symphony
Painting
Photography
Play
Playwright
Poetry
Prose
Quilting
Screenplay
Sculpture
Videography
Musical

MUSICAL INSTRUMENTS

Accordion
Bagpipes
Banjo
Baritone horn

Bass
Bass drum
Bass guitar
Bells

Bugle
Calliope
Castanets
Cello
Clarinet
Coronet
Cymbals
Electric guitar
English horn
Fiddle
Fife
Flute
French horn
Guitar
Harmonica
Harp
Harpsichord
Lyre
Mandolin

Mellophone
Oboe
Organ
Percussion
Piano
Piccolo
Pipe organ
Saxophone
Snare drum
Tambourine
Triangle
Trombone
Trumpet
Tuba
Tympani
Ukulele
Viola
Violin
Xylophone

CHARITIES/ORGANIZATIONS & FUND RAISING

Is one of your characters a philanthropist? What about having your hero or heroine interested in donating to a certain charity or participating in a walk-a-thon? This list is a great place to find an organization to match a character's desire to contribute or their need for service.

ORGANIZATIONS, CHARITIES, ETC.

350.org
Academy of American Poets
Action Against Hunger
Acton Institute for the Study of Religion and Liberty
Alex's Lemonade Stand Foundation
Alley Cat Allies
ALS Association
ALSAC—St. Jude's Children Research Hospital
Alzheimer's Association
American Association for the Advancement of Science
American Cancer Society
American Civil Liberties Union Foundation
American Diabetes Association
American Enterprise Institute for Public Policy Research
American Foundation for Suicide Prevention
American Heart Association
American Humanist Association
American Lung Association
American Museum of Natural History

American Red Cross
American Society for the Prevention of Cruelty to Animals
Americares
Andrew Wommack Ministries
Animal Legal Defense Fund
Animal Welfare Institute
Appalachian Mountain Club
Appalachian Trail Conservancy
Arthritis Foundation
Ashoka
Autism Action
Best Friends Animal Society
Big Brother Big Sister
Bill & Melinda Gates Foundation
Boys & Girls Clubs of America
Brain Injury Alliance
Breast cancer fund-raising
Brennan Center for Justice at NYU School of Law
Cancer Research Institute
CARE
Carnegie Endowment for International Peace
Catholic Charities USA
Center for Biological Diversity
Center for Reproductive Rights
Charity: Water
Children International
Cincinnati Zoo & Botanical Garden
Clearwater Marine Aquarium
Comic Relief
Committee to Protect Journalists
Compassion International
Conservation International
Council on Foreign Relations
Creative Commons

Cystic Fibrosis Foundation
Cystic Fibrosis Research, Inc.
Dana-Farber Cancer Institute
Direct Relief
Disabled American Veterans Charitable Service Trust
Do Something
Doctors Without Borders
Domestic abuse shelters
DonorsChoose.org
Economic Policy Institute
Equal Justice Initiative
FAIR Federation for American Immigration Reform
Feeding America
Focus on the Family
Food and Water Watch
Free Software Foundation
Friends of the Earth
Give.org
GiveWell
GlobalGiving
GuideStar
Guttmacher Institute
Habitat for Humanity
Help for Heroes
Homeless shelters
Houston Zoo
Human Rights Watch
International Rescue Committee
Khan Academy
Kiva
Kiwanis International
KQED
Leukemia & Lymphoma Society
Lincoln Center for the Performing Arts

Lion's Club
Make-A-Wish Foundation
MAP International
March of Dimes
Metropolitan Museum of Art
Michael J. Fox Foundation for Parkinson's Research
Muscular Dystrophy Association
Museum of Fine Arts, Boston
NAMI
NARAL Pro-Choice America Foundation
National Audubon Society
National Council of YMCAs of the USA
National Immigration Law Center
National Multiple Sclerosis Society
National Pediatric Cancer Foundation
National Women's Law Center
Natural Resources Defense Council
Navy SEAL Foundation
New York City Ballet
NPR
Ocean Conservancy
Oceana
Oxfam
Partners in Health
PBS
Philadelphia Museum of Art
Planned Parenthood Federation of America
Rainforest Action Network
Reading is Fundamental
Ronald McDonald House Charities
Safe Kids Worldwide
Saint Louis Zoo Association
Samaritan's Purse
San Diego Zoo Global

Save the Children
Smithsonian Institution
Southern Poverty Law Center
Special Olympics
Statue of Liberty-Ellis Island Foundation
StoryCorps
Sundance Institute
Susan G. Komen for the Cure
Teach for America
The Atlantic Council of the United States
The Carter Center
The Center for Strategic and International Studies
The Climate Reality Project
The John F. Kennedy Center for the Performing Arts
The Museum of Modern Art
The Nature Conservancy
The Public Theater/New York Shakespeare Festival
The Rotary Foundation of Rotary International
The Salvation Army
The Trevor Project
UNICEF
Union of Concerned Scientists
United Nations Foundation
United Way
Veterans of Foreign Wars Foundation
Wikimedia Foundation
Wildlife Conservation Network
Wildlife Conservation Society
World Resources Institute
World Vision
World Wildlife Fund
Wounded Warrior Project
YMCA
Young Life

FUND-RAISING CAUSES FOR YOUR CHARACTER

4-H
Academic Decathlon
Academic Triathlon
African American Student Alliance
American Mathematics Competitions
American Regions Math League
American Sign Language Club
Amnesty International
Animal rights club
Animation
Anime/manga club
Architecture club
Art sculpting and multi-media
Art: drawing, painting
Astronomy club
Biology club
Blogging
Book club
Boy Scouts
Breast Cancer Awareness
Cancer Foundation
Caribou Mathematics Competition
Cartooning
Ceramics
Chamber music group
Chemistry club
Chemistry Olympiad
Chess club
Chinese club
Choreography
Church choir
Church groups

Civil Air Patrol
Classic film club
Clean Tech Competition
Comedy club
Comic book/game clubs
Community chorus/choir
Community festivals
Community government
Community theater program
Community youth board
Concert band
Creative Communication Poetry Contest
Dance
Debate club
Distributive Education Clubs of America (DECA)
Drama club
Dungeons and Dragons club
Eco club
Eco-Challenge
Economics club
Electronics club
Engineering club
English as a Second Language club
English club
Ensembles
Entrepreneurship club
Environmental club
Equestrian club
Ethics club
Euro Challenge
Fair trade club
Fan fiction club
Fashion design
Fellowship of Christian Athletes

Film production club
FIRST Robotics Competition
Foreign Affairs Club
Fraternities and sororities
French club
Future Business Leaders of America
Future Farmers of America
Gamers club
Gavels club
Gay-Straight Alliance
Geocaching club
Gender-Sexuality Alliance
German club
Girl Scouts
Girls Lean International
Graphic design
High School Fed Challenge
High School Innovation Challenge
High school sports teams/extra-curricular activities
High school theater group
High school theater program
History club
Homeowners associations
Horticulture club
Intel International Science and Engineering Fair
International food club
International Thespian Society
Jazz band
Jewelry making
Jewish Student Union
Junior ROTC
Junior Statesmen of America
JUNTOS
Key club

Kids Helping Kids
Kids Philosophy Slam
Language clubs
LARPing (Live Action Role Playing)
Latin club
Leo club
Life sciences club
Literary magazine club
Literature club
Marching band
Math club
Math Honor Society
Math League
Math team
Miming
Missionary work
Mock Trial Club
Model railroads
Model United Nations
Mountaineers club
Music Honor Society
National Academic Quiz Tournament
National Art Society
National Beta Club
National Business Honor Society
National French Contest
National History Bee
National Honor Society
National Technology Honor Society
NOW (National Organization for Women)
Nursing home or hospital volunteer club
Odyssey of the Mind
Orchestra
Pacific Islanders Club

Peer Leadership Group
Peer tutoring
Photography club
Physics club
Poetry club
Poetry Out Loud
Pokémon/Pokémon Go club
Psychology club
Puppetry
Questions Unlimited
Quill and Scroll
Quiz Bowl
Renaissance fairs
Robotics club
Russian club
SADD (Students Against Destructive Decisions)
Scholar Bowl
School chorus/choir
School newspaper/newsletter
School or local magazine/journal/newspaper
School or local radio station
School or local television channel
School or local website
Science bowl
Science fair
Science National Honors Society
Science Olympiad
Scripps National Spelling Bee
Sculpture
Sewing
Singing club
Slam poetry club
Social media
Solo music

Soup kitchen volunteer
South Asian Student Society
Spanish club
Spanish Honor Society
Speech and debate club
Student council
Student Diplomacy Corps
Teenage Republicans
The Civil War Reenactors
Thespian Society
Tri-M Music Honor Society
Trivia and quiz clubs
Video game development club
Weaving
Web designing-coding clubs
Woodworking
Work on a movie
Writing club
Yearbook club
Yearbook committee
YMCA Youth and Government
Young Democrats of America
Youth and government clubs
Youth groups

FUND-RAISING ACTIVITIES

10,000 step challenge
10,000 stair steps challenge
50/50 raffle
5K run/walk
Art classes
Art sale
Awareness bracelets

Babysitting
Backyard barbecue
Bake sale
Bar crawl
Baseball fund-raiser
Basketball fund-raiser
Bingo
Board game tournament
Book donations
Book swap
Bottle deposit donation
Bowling for bucks
Can collection
Car wash
Carnival
Caroling for a cause
Change (coins) drive
Charity auctions
Charity chores
Cheerleader fund-raiser
Chili cook-off
Christmas tree delivery
Clothing donations
Clothing sale
Coffee donation
Cold water plunge
Community picnic
Community yard sale
Company match
Concert
Cookbook
Cooking/baking contest
Craft fair
Create and sell calendars

Create custom T-shirts
Croquet tournament
Crowdfunding
Dance
Date night auction
Dodgeball tournament
Dollars for dares
Donation collection—food
Donation collection—money
Donation kiosks
Donation match drive
Dunk tank
Easter egg hunt
Face painting
Fantasy football
Fashion show
Field day
Fitness class
Flash mob
Food truck event
Fund raising cards
Funky clothes challenge
Gala
Game night
Giving tree
Golf marathon/tournament
Grilling/BBQ contest
Grocery delivery
Grow a beard
Guest speaker
Happy hour
Haunted house
Hockey fund-raiser
Holiday cookie swap

Holiday flower sale
Holiday fund raising
Hoops for Hope
Host a kid's camp
Hot cocoa sale
Hug booth
Hunger bowl
Hunger challenge
Ice cream social
In-house competitions
Jeans day/dress down Friday
Karaoke
Kickball tournament
Lemonade stand
Little league fund-raiser
Local artists' auction
Local celebrity appearance
Local restaurant sponsorships
Marathon
March Madness bracket
Marches (March of Dimes, etc.)
Movie night
Murder mystery dinner
Museum night
Obstacle course
Olympic games
Online auction
Online donations
Online fund-raiser
Online petition
Pitch-a-thon
Ornament swap
Outrageous bet for charity
Personal challenge
Phone-a-thon

Photo booth
Photo contest
Pie in the face
Ping pong tournament
Pitch-a-thon
Pool party
Potluck
Prime parking spot
Raffle
Rent-an-athlete fund-raiser
Rock-a-thon (rocking chair)
Rubber duck race
Santa
Scavenger hunt
Scratch cards
Selling trees/saplings
Serve-a-thon
Shave head
Silent auctions
Singing valentines/telegrams
Skip meals
Skydiving
Soccer fund-raiser
Softball fund-raiser
Supervisor rental
Swim-a-thon
Talent show
Tennis fund-raiser
Text donations
Thermometer fund-raiser
Track fund-raiser
Tree planting party
Trivia tournament
Variety show
Varsity fund-raiser

Vehicle donation
Viral video challenge
Volleyball fund-raiser
Wacky sports tournament
Walk-and-paw-a-thon
Walk/run
Water balloon fight

Weight loss-a-thon
Work-a-thon
Workout challenge
Wreaths and wrapping
Yard/garage/neighborhood sale
Zoo night

DATING OR FUN WITH FRIENDS

Adopt a pet from an animal shelter together and/or play with puppies
Adventure night
Airport: get soonest departing flight to anywhere, stay for a weekend
All day getaway
Aquarium
Arcade
Archery
Aromatherapy night
Art classes
Art exhibits
Arts festival
Autumn festival
Autumn leaf hunting
Bake a pie or mini pies
Bake and decorate homemade cookies
Bake dessert from scratch
Bake holiday treats
Bake sale
Barbecue with friends
Barn dance
Beer tasting at brewery
Bike ride
Bike ride through fall foliage
Binge-watch a TV show
Bingo night together
Bonfire
Book last minute getaway
Bookstore date
Bowling

Breakfast or brunch
Build a model or work of art together
Build a snowman and drink hot cocoa
Build something for your home
Build something together
Camping
Candlelit dinner at home, special occasion serving pieces, dress up
Canoe or kayak
Card games
Carnival
Car show
Check coupon sites for new and interesting activities
Chili cook-off
Church festival
Coffee shop
Coffee shops: hit every one in town
Color adult coloring books
Coloring contest
Comedy club—open mic or improv
Community day
Community or school orchestra or symphony
Community play
Cook together
Cooking contest
County fair
Cozy up to the fireplace
Craft class
Crafts and shows
Create a backyard escape to enjoy together
Crossword contest
Decorate a gingerbread house together
Dinner party
Do a puzzle
Do lamest tour in area that you have secretly been wanting to do

Dress up in formal attire and attend classical concert or opera
Drive around to see Christmas lights
Drive somewhere unknown, dinner in city never been to, use fake names
Drive-in movie
Estate, yard sale, garage sale, flea market, searching for "treasures"
Farmer's market
Feed birds or ducks at nearby lake
Festivals such as wine, ethnic foods, chocolate, Taco Day
Fireworks
Fishing
Flip through photo albums
Fly kites
Fondue
Foodie tour
Four wheeling
Frisbee
Fruit picking
Game night
Geocaching
Get lost in a corn maze, no map allowed
Ghost tour
Go for a manicure or pedicure together
Go-carting
Greek festival
Hammocking
Happy hour
Haunted house
Head to snow and do snow activities
Help the needy
High school homecoming game
High school or college play
Hike to a waterfall
Hiking
Hit golf balls at driving range

Hockey game
Holiday parade
Holiday picnic at the park
Horse drawn carriage ride
Host a holiday party
Host a tropical party
Host a wine and cheese party
Hot air ballooning
Hot tub/spa date night
Ice cream date
Indoor gun range
Indoor mini golfing
Indoor paint ball
Inside or outside picnic
International grocery store
Invite friends and play board games
Jazz concert
Jenga
Karaoke
Kickboxing or karate class
Korean BBQ
Laser tag
Learn a foreign or sign language
Learn about your town's history
Live music
Local band
Long walk
Make a fort together
Make a scarecrow
Make a scrapbook together
Make caramel and candy apples
Make Chinese food at home
Make decorations at home
Make homemade pizza

Make mulled wine

Make photolog of a day in the life of an invisible man using boots

Make your own holiday cards

Massage night

Meditate together

Midnight movie

Mine tour

Mini weekend road trip

Mountain top: star gaze with lots of blankets to snuggle under

Movie in theater

Movie marathon at home with popcorn and sundaes

Movies in the park

Murder mystery group date

Murder mystery theatre

Museum

Musical

Mystery date. Place selections in envelopes and pick at random.

National park

Nerf gunfight

No technology for whole day

Opera

Outdoor concert

Paddleboat

Paint a picture of spring together

Paint a room

Paint each other's portraits

Paint pottery

Parade in the city

Park

Penny slots at casino and take advantage of free drinks

People watch in mall or in coffee shop and make up stories about them

Photo shoot

Photograph your city

Pick a pumpkin at pumpkin patch

Play 20 questions
Play a board or video game together
Play a sport
Play basketball
Play bird watching bingo
Play board games at coffee shop
Play goofy golf
Play on a playground
Play ping-pong
Play tennis
Play truth or dare
Poetry reading
Popcorn balls
Pretend to be a tourist and see hometown sights/sites
Professional orchestra and symphony
Psychic reading
Queso making
Re-arrange a room
Read a book together or out loud to each other
Read ghost stories
Recline by the pool
Rent an old movie and put on mute. Improvise dialogue
Research local trains
Road trip
Rock climbing
Roller skating or ice-skating
Rollerblading
Romantic dinner at home
Scavenger hunt
Seasonal activities: tree decorating, pumpkin carving, coloring Easter eggs
See your favorite band in concert
Shop together and find each other a gift for under $25
Sky diving
Snowboarding

Social club
Spa night together
Spend a rainy day in a museum or aquarium
Sports game
Spring/Summer/Fall/Winter festivals
Stargazing
Start a garden
Start workout routine together
Staycation at local B&B or Inn and play tourist
Strip poker
Sweater weather picnic
Swimming pool
Take a class together of a common interest
Take a community education class together
Take a cooking class
Take dance lessons together
Take dog for a walk
Teach each other about something you do that they want to learn
Theme night such as everything Mexican from food to movies
Theme park
Throw a football around at park, repping different football teams
Tour local gardens
Trivia night at local bar
Try a new restaurant
Uno
Video game showdown
Visit a castle
Visit a factory, like a chocolate one
Visit a historic small town together
Visit an old church
Visit children in hospitals
Visit downtown
Visit open homes and discuss your dream home
Visit retirement homes

Visit the boardwalk
Visit the library
Visit the oldest graveyard in the city
Volunteer together
Volunteer at a soup kitchen
Walk around your town
Watch all movies nominated the current year up for an Oscar
Watch funny YouTube videos
Watch planes at the airport
Watch scary movies together
Watch sports at a bar and cheer for your team
Watch the sunrise
Watch the sunset
Water gun or water balloon fight
Water skiing
Water park
Whitewater rafting
Window shopping
Winery or brewery tour
Work out together
Write a letter to each other in the future
Write a seasonal bucket list together
Write fiction together at an outside cafe
Yoga
Zip-lining
Zoo

HOBBIES

HOBBIES—INDOOR

Amateur radio
Animation
Astrology
Baking
Board/tabletop games
Bonsai tree
Book art
Book restoration
Building sets
Calligraphy
Candle making
Coloring
Cooking
Cosplaying
Crocheting
Cross-stitch
Crossword puzzles
Cryptography
Dance
Digital arts
Drawing
Embroidery
Fantasy sports
Fishkeeping
Flower arranging
Fused glass
Gaming

Genealogy
Glassblowing
Graphic design
Gunsmithing
Homebrewing
Hydroponics
Jewelry making
Jigsaw puzzles
Juggling
Knitting
Leather crafting
Lego building
Magic
Metalworking
Miniature trains
Model building
Needlepoint
Origami
Painting
Photography
Playing musical instruments
Quilting
Reading
Robotics
Scrapbooking
Sculpting
Sewing

Shopping
Singing
Sketching
Soapmaking
Stand-up comedy
Table tennis
Taxidermy
Video editing

Video gaming
Watching movies
Watching television
Wood carving
Woodworking
Writing
Yoga

HOBBIES—OUTDOOR

Air sports
Astronomy
Backpacking/hiking
Beekeeping
Birdwatching
Blacksmithing
Butterfly watching
Camping
Dog sledding
Dowsing
Fishing
Flag football
Flying
Flying disc
Gardening
Geocaching
Ghost hunting
Gold prospecting
Graffiti
Hiking
Hooping
Horseback riding
Hunting

Inline skating
Kite flying
Metal detecting
People watching
Photography
Rocketry
Sailing
Sand art
Scouting
Shooting
Shopping
Spelunking
Steeplechase
Stone skipping
Storm chasing
Sunbathing
Topiary
Travel
Urban exploration
Vacation
Vehicle restoration
Volunteering
Walking

HOBBIES—COLLECTION

Action figures

Antiques

Art glass

Artwork

Books

Buttons

Cards

Coins

Comic books

Die-cast toys

Dolls

Figurines

Flower collecting and pressing

Fossils

Insects

Knives

Minerals

Movie and movie memorabilia

Rail transport modeling

Records

Sea glass

Seashells

Shoes

Stamps

Stone

Swords

Tools

Toys

Video games

Vintage cars

SPORTS

Auto racing
Baseball
Basketball
Beach volleyball
Bowling
Broomball
Canadian football
Cheerleading
Cricket
Cross-country running
Curling
Dance team
Field hockey
Fives
Foosball
Football
Handball
Hockey
Hurling
Ice cricket
Ice hockey
Indoor field hockey

Inline hockey
Lacrosse
Laser tag
Medley swimming
Polo
Quidditch club
Relay racing
Roller derby
Roller inline hockey
Rounders
Rowing
Rugby football
Soccer
Softball
Sport wrestling
Street hockey
Tug of war
Volleyball
Water polo
Wheelchair curling
Wheelchair handball
Wrestling

INDIVIDUAL

Alpine skiing
Archery
Arm wrestling
Ballet

BASE jumping
Bobsled
Bodyboarding
Bodybuilding

Bowling
Boxing
Bungee jumping
Canoeing
Caving
Cheerleading
Chess
Cliff scaling
Climbing
Cross-country skiing
CrossFit
Cycling
Dancing
Darts
Discus
Diving
Fencing
Fishing
Freediving
Gliding
Golf
Gymnastics
Hang gliding
Hiking
Horse racing
Horse riding
Hunting with bow
Hunting with rifle
Ice climbing
Jet ski
Kayaking
Kitesurfing
Long-distance jumping
Longboarding

Luge
Lumberjack sports
Marathon running
Martial arts
Monster truck
Motocross
Motorcycling
Motorsports
Mountain biking
Mountain climbing
Paintball
Parachuting
Paragliding
Parasailing
Ping pong
Poker
Pole vaulting
Pool
Powerlifting
Racquetball
Rafting
Rappelling
Rodeo
Running
Scuba diving
Shot put
Skateboarding
Skating
Skeet shooting
Ski jumping
Skiing
Sledding
Snorkeling
Snow skiing

Snowboarding
Surfing
Swimming
Table tennis
Taekwondo
Tennis
Toboggan
Track and field
Triathlon

Ultimate Frisbee
Wakeboarding
Water polo
Water skiing
Wave ski
Weightlifting
Wrestling
Yoga
Zip-line

MARTIAL ARTS

Aikido
Hapkido
Judo
Jujutsu
Kajukenbo
Karate

Kickboxing
Krav Maga
Mixed martial arts
Muay Thai
Taekwondo

TOYS & GAMES

CARD GAMES

52 pickup
500
Beggar-my-neighbor
Bezique
Bieten
Bisca
Bohemian Schneider
Canasta
Cards Against Humanity
Casino
Crazy 8s
Cribbage
Écarté
Egyptian Ratscrew
Elfern
Exploding Kittens
Gaigel
German Rummy
Gin rummy
Karnöffel
Klaberjass
Marjolet
Minchiate
Officers' Skat

Old Maid
Oma Skat
Perlaggen
Pinochle
Piquet
Poker
Rummy
Schnapsen
Schrum-Schrum
Sedma
Shithead
Sixty-Six
Solitaire
Speed
Spit
Spoons
Strohmandeln
Svoyi Koziri
Tarocchini
Unteransetzen
Viennese Rummy
War
Watten
Zwickern

POKER GAMES

2-7 triple draw	HORSE
5-card draw	Omaha
7-card stud	Razz
Chinese poker	Texas Hold'em

BOARD GAMES/DOMINOES, ETC.

7 Wonders	Descent: Journeys in the Dark
A Game of Thrones	Diplomacy
Acquire	Dixit
Agricola	Dominant Species
Alhambra	Dominion
Apples to Apples	Dominoes
Arkham Horror	Don't Break the Ice
Axis and Allies	Dungeon!
Backgammon	El Grande
Balderdash	Go
Battleship	Guess Who?
Battlestar Galactica	Hi Ho! Cherry-O
Blood Bowl	Key to the Kingdom
Candyland	Le Havre
Carcassonne	Mahjong
Cards Against Humanity	Mancala
Caylus	Mastermind
Checkers	Monopoly
Chess	Operation
Chinese Checkers	Pandemic
Chutes and Ladders	Parcheesi
Clue	Pay Day
Connect Four	Pictionary
Cosmic Encounter	Power Grid
Cranium	Puerto Rico

Reversi/Othello
Risk
Say Anything
Scattergories
Scotland Yard
Scrabble
Settlers of Catan
Shadows Over Camelot
Shogun
Smallworld
Sorry!
Stratego
Summoner Wars
Taboo

The Game of Life
The Invasion of Canada
Through the Ages
Ticket to Ride
Tigris and Euphrates
Trivial Pursuit
Trouble
Twilight Imperium
Twilight Struggle
Uno
Uno Attack
Wits and Wagers
Yahtzee

INDOOR GAMES

Animal charades
Bigger than a breadbox
Bubbles
Charades
Coloring books
Connect four
Crab walk
Darts
Dice games
Domino toppling
Duck, duck, goose
Hide and seek
Hot potato
I Spy
I've-got-a-secret
Indoor basketball
Indoor bowling

Indoor croquet
Indoor mini golf
Indoor obstacle course
Jenga
Keep the balloon up
Legos
Lincoln Logs
Marbles
Mirror, mirror
Musical chairs
Obstacle maze
Paper airplanes
Paper dolls
Pick-up sticks
Pillowcase race
Pillow fort
Ping pong

Ping pong ball catch
Puzzles
Race cars/tracks
Rock, paper, scissors
Scavenger hunt

Simon Says
Table hockey
Table shuffleboard
Twenty Questions
Twister

OUTDOOR GAMES

Angry Birds
Bean bag toss
Bird watching
Boat races
Bubble blowing
Capture the flag
Catch
Chinese jump rope
Cloud watching
Croquet
Dodge ball
Don't drop the ball
Double Dutch
Firefly chasing
Hopscotch
HORSE
Horseshoes
Hula hoop
Juggle
Jump rope
Kick the can
Kickball

Kite flying
Lawn bowling
Limbo
Mini golf
Mother May I
Obstacle course
Red light green light
Red rover
Safari
Sandbox
Scavenger hunt
Shuffleboard
Simon Says
Skipping rocks
Sprinkler running
Tag
Three-legged race
Tree climbing
Tug of War
Water balloons
Water guns

CHILDREN'S TOYS/GIFTS—QUICK LIST

Action figures

Archery set

Art set
Baking kit
Binoculars
Construction toys
Dinosaurs
Drones
Drum set
Electronic tablet
Emergency vehicle toys
Gardening kit
Guitar
Headphones
Hoverboard
Jewelry making kits
Kick scooter
Legos
Magic tricks
Maze puzzle

Microscope
Mini drones
Model kits
Musical instruments
Playhouse
Racing cars
Remote control car
Robot
Science kit
Skateboard
Space educational craft toy
Spinning top
Sports sets
Telescope
Toolkit
Video games
Walkie Talkies

CHILDREN'S TOYS—NOSTALGIC

Baby Alive
Baby Tender Love
Barbie
Beanie Babies
Cabbage Patch Kids
Chatty Cathy
Easy-Bake Oven
Etch-A-Sketch
Furby
G.I. Joe
Hotwheels
Hula Hoop
Koosh ball

Legos
Matchbox cars
Mr. Potato Head
My Little Pony
Nerf
Play-Doh
Radio Flyer
Rubik's Cube
Silly Putty
Simon
Slinky
Stretch Armstrong
Teddy Ruxpin

Teenage Mutant Ninja Turtles
Tickle Me Elmo
Transformers

View-Master
Weeble
Yo-yos

VIDEO GAMES—POPULAR & NOSTALGIC

Angry Birds
Anthem
Assassin's Creed
Banjo-Kazooie
Battlefield 1942
BioShock
Call of Duty
Counter-Strike
Dark Souls
Destiny
Diablo
Donkey Kong
Doom
Fallout
Far Cry
Final Fantasy
Fortnite
God of War
Grand Theft Auto
Half-Life
Halo
League of Legends
Madden NFL
Mario Brothers
Mass Effect
Mega Man
Metal Gear Solid
Metroid Prime

Minecraft
Monster Hunter
Ms. Pac-Man
Overwatch
Pac-Man
Pokémon
Pokémon Go
Pong
Red Dead Redemption
Resident Evil
Rock Band
Shadow of the Colossus
SimCity
Sonic the Hedgehog
Soulcalibur
Space Invaders
Spider-Man
StarCraft
Street Fighter
Super Mario
Super Metroid
Super Smash Brothers
Tetris
The Elder Scrolls
The Legend of Zelda
Uncharted
World of Warcraft

OCCUPATIONS

One of the first questions usually asked when meeting someone new is "What do you do?" A person's occupation defines him or her, creating first impressions whether positive or negative or even neutral. It should be one of the first traits, not the last, to add to your characterization.

Don't underestimate your character's occupation. It can increase power to your story, change the direction of your plot or create an unexpected twist. Occupations can also add depth to your character and reveal that person's motivations.

A character's occupation can deepen varying levels of conflict. Imagine an accountant who hates math, a national speaker frightened of large crowds, or a pilot terrified of flying. A character's occupation can also open certain doors unavailable to others. A schoolteacher or accountant is going to have a more challenging time investigating a neighbor, new lover or secretive family member than a detective or police officer would. Such a scenario can create conflict for your character.

There are stereotypes for every job. A homicide police officer with decades of experience can be seen as jaded, humorless and sarcastic. A librarian probably brings to mind someone who loves the written word, dislikes crowds or loud events, and sees a book as highly entertaining. As a writer, you can play up those stereotypes or give them opposite traits.

The plot can veer into different directions through a character's occupation. What if a high-powered attorney's life involves eighty-hour workweeks, with no time for personal pursuits, and she's close to having a nervous breakdown from complete exhaustion? All those factors can propel your character into various choices. She can take drastic measures by quitting, retaliating against her company or boss, admitting herself into a psychiatric ward. Or she can continue to take it and lose everyone around her she loves.

Writing about a character who is out of his element when it comes to his career choice can show varying degrees of his personality. What about a police detective who is thrust into a violent case involving a serial killer? What about a professor's first day at her job? Occupations can add humor or horror and everything in between. What if your character owns a coffee shop but makes an awful cup of coffee and even hates the stuff? Where can she go from there? Or maybe she doesn't know she makes terrible coffee because her employees are too afraid to say anything?

A person's job can reveal a lack of character. Picture an accountant embezzling money from the company, a veterinarian who is abusive to animals, a social worker with little or no empathy, or a computer repairman who installs spyware. A job can also show a character rising above.

The following comprehensive lists can ignite ideas of what your character does during the day or as a side hobby. They include hundreds of occupations to choose from, all broken down by industry.

OCCUPATIONS BY CATEGORY

AGRICULTURE

Agricultural engineer

Agriculture inspector

Agronomist

Animal biotechnologist

Animal geneticist

Animal physical therapist

Animal welfare specialist

Apiary worker

Arborist

Artificial insemination technician

Bioinformatics scientist

Bioprocessing engineer

Breeding manager

Cowboy

Crop adjuster

Crop advisor

Crop specialist

Dairy farm worker

Embryologist

Entomologist

Extension agent

Farm supply representative

Farmer

Farrier

Fermentation scientist

Fertilizer sales representative

Food engineer

Game warden

Grain buyer

Grain marketing specialist

Greenhouse manager

Herdsman

Horse trainer

Horticulturist

Hydroponics producer

Irrigation engineer

Livestock auctioneer

Livestock buyer

Livestock feedlot operator

Livestock hauler

Machine design engineer

Meat inspector

Plant biologist

Plant breeder

Plant geneticist

Poultry hatchery manager

Produce buyer

Produce inspector

Ranch foreman

Ranch manager

Rancher

Sanitary/waste handling

Soil conservationist

Soil scientist

Soil surveyor
Structural engineer

Tractor operator
Zoologist

ANIMALS

Animal control officer
Animal cruelty investigator
Animal nutritionist
Animal research technologist
Animal shelter manager
Animal trainer
Animal trainers—entertainment
Animal welfare auditor
Animal welfare compliance
Aquarist
Aquarium designer
Dog or cat breeder
Dog sitting
Dog trainer
Dog walker
Equine veterinarian
Groomer
Kennel tech
Laboratory technician
Marine biologist
Pampered pet

Park naturalist
Pet adoption counselor
Pet sitter
Pet store supplies
Pooper scooper
Pound
Rescue
Seeing-eye dog trainer
Vet tech
Veterinarian
Veterinary dentist
Veterinary pathologist
Wildlife economist
Wildlife educator
Wildlife inspector
Wildlife manager
Wildlife photographer
Wildlife rehabilitator
Wolf biologist
Zoo veterinarian
Zoologist

ART

3D modeling
Advertising photography
Aerial photography
Airbrushing
Animation and effects

Animator
Anime
Architecture
Art auctioneer
Art dealer

Art history

Art professor

Art teacher

Art therapy

Augmented reality game design

Basket weaving

Book illustration

Canvas

Caricature art

Cartoon art

Cartoonist

Comic book art

Computer animation

Costume design

Courtroom sketch artist

Cover artist

Craft art

Fabric dyeing

Fine artist

Glass art

Glass blowing

Graffiti art

Handblown glass

Illustrator

Knitting/crochet

Logo design

Macrame

Macro photography

Manga

Medical illustration

Mosaic art

Multi-media

Muralist

Museum curator

Museum exhibit design

Nature photography

Needlework

Painting

Pen and ink/pencil drawings

Photographer

Photojournalist

Portrait art

Portrait photography

Pottery

Print design

Printmaker

Product design

Quilting

Role-Playing Game Design

Screen-printing

Sculptor—clay

Sculptor—glass

Sculptor—ice

Sculptor—metal

Sculptor—scrap

Sculptor—stone/marble/granite

Sculptor—wood

Sewing

Ship/model building

Sketching

Stained glass

Storyboard artist

Studio arts

Tatting/making lace

Tattoo art

Teacher/university lecturer

Textile design

Tie-dye

Underwater photography
Video game design
Visual effects

Weaving
Wedding photography
Woodworking

ATHLETICS

Assistant athletic trainer
Assistant coach
Associate athletic director
Athlete
Athletic program development dir.
Athletic trainer
Athletics director
Baseball coach
Basketball coach
Business manager
Coach
Cruise ship recreation manager
Director of Community Relations
Dir. of Minor League Operations
Doctor of Osteopathy
Equipment manager
Event coordinator
Exercise physiologist
Football coach
General manager
High school coach
Kinesiotherapist
Marketing director
Personal trainer
Physical education (P.E.) teacher
Physical therapist
Physical therapy assistant
Promotion director

Public address announcer
Public relations
Public relations assistant
Sales representative
Scoreboard operator
Scout
Soccer coach
Softball coach
Sport court design
Sports and fitness nutritionist
Sports announcer/commentator
Sports columnist
Sports editor
Sports events coordinator
Sports executive
Sports intern
Sports journalism
Sports marketing
Sports massage therapist
Sports medicine aide
Sports nutritionist/dietician
Sports photographer
Sports physical therapist
Sports physician
Sports psychologist
Sports publisher
Sports radio show host
Sports reporter

Sports talk show host
Sports television producer
Sportswriter
Stadium manager

Strength and conditioning coach
Ticket operations manager
Traveling assistant
Volleyball coach

EDUCATION

Admissions counselor
Admissions director
Adult education
Art teacher
Associate professor
Audiovisual librarian
Automotive instructor
Biology teacher
Career center
Childcare aide
Childcare teacher
Chinese teacher
College president
College professor
College recruiter
Computer science teacher
Continuing education
Custodian
Dean of students
Dental school
Department head
Distance education
Distance education program director
Driver's education instructor
Early childhood teacher
Education administrator
Education consultant

Elementary school teacher
English teacher
ESL teacher
French teacher
German teacher
Graduate
High school teacher
Historian
History teacher
Information technology
Instructor
International student advisor
Journalism teacher
Kindergarten teacher
Latin teacher
Library director
Literacy teacher
Maintenance
Math teacher
Media library specialist
Middle school teacher
Montessori teacher
Music teacher
Nursing
Online instructor
Optometry
P.E. teacher

Placement counselor
Preschool teacher
Principal
Professor
Reference librarian
School administrator
School board
School counselor
School librarian
School nurse
School psychologist
School secretary
Science teacher
Secondary school teacher
Social studies teacher

Spanish teacher
Special ed teacher
Student counselor
Substitute teacher
Summer schoolteacher
Superintendent
Teacher
Teacher's aid
Teaching assistant
Tutoring
Undergraduate
Vice principal
Vocational instructor
Writing teacher

EMERGENCY SERVICES

911 operator
Ambulance driver
Assistant Dir. of Emergency Services
Bomb disposal
Cave rescue
Certified nursing assistant
Coast Guard
Counterterrorism
Director of emergency services
Disaster preparedness
Disaster response
Disaster management
Emergency communications
Emergency disaster management
Emergency management
Emergency physician

Emergency preparedness
Emergency road service
Emergency room physician
Emergency Room RN
Emergency services coordinator
Emergency medical technician
ER physician
Fire and rescue
Firefighter
Fire inspector
Fire protection engineer
Fire safety director
First responder
Hot Shots
ICU nurse
K9

K9 handler
Licensed practical nurse EMS
Lifeguard
Med tech EMS
Mine rescue
Mountain rescue
Nurse practitioner EMS
Paramedic transport
Pediatric emergency medicine
Poison control

Police
Physician's assistant EMS
Receptionist/concierge EMT certified
Registered nurse EMS
Search and rescue
Security F/T fire safety director
Travel EMS nurse
Ultrasound EMS
Vehicle extrication
Volunteer fire department

ENTERTAINMENT

Actor—commercials
Actor—movies/big screen
Actor—TV
Animal trainer
Animation director
Animation/graphic design/FX
Animator
Anime
Art director
Audio engineer technician
Ballet
Ballroom dancers
Booking agent
Boom operator
Buddy films
Carnival worker
Casino
Casting director
Celebrity photographer
Chick flicks
Choreographer

Cinematographer
Circus performer
Comedy
Concert promoter
Construction manager
Costume designer
Crew jobs
Critic
Dealers
Development executive
Dialect coach
Digital creative consultant
Director
Director of Photography
Disc jockey
Dog handler
Drama
Entertainment attorney
Film and video editor
Film director
Film editing

Film hair stylist
Gaffer
Gaming book writer
Grip
Horror
Illustrator
Improv
Licensing representative
Lighting technician
Location manager
Makeup artist
Mixing engineer
Music journalist
Music publisher
Music soundtracks
Music therapist
Musician
Opera singer
Paparazzi
Performing artist
Playwriting
Pole dancer
Producer
Production assistant
Production designer
Prop maker
Publicist
Recording engineer
Romantic comedy

Sales/marketing consultant
Salsa
Screenwriting
Scriptwriters
Set decorator
Set design
Sitcoms
Sound effects
Sound effects editor
Sports book writer
Stand-up comedian
Studio chef
Stunt performer
Talent agent
Tango
Tap dancer
Television editor
Television floor manager
Television producer
Theater consultant
Theater director
Thriller
Trapeze artist
Ventriloquist
Video editing
Voice actor
Voice over
Writer

FOOD

Appliance and technology tester
Artisan bread baker

Banquets
Bartender

Bed and breakfast owner
Boutique chef
Busboy
Butcher
Cake decorating
Caterer
Celebrity chef
Cheese connoisseur
Cheese maker
Coffee shop owner
Cookbook author
Cooking contest judge
Cooking school owner
Craft brewer
Cruise ship chef
Culinary artist
Culinary school instructor
Deli owner
Dietician
Dishwasher
Executive chef
Farm to fork mobile truck
Farmer's market manager
Fast food
Fine dining
Food blogger
Food critic
Food gift basket maker
Food labeling specialist
Food lawyer
Food newsletter producer
Food photographer
Food product development scientist
Food safety auditor

Food scientist
Food stylist
Food writer
Hole in the wall owner
Holistic health coach
Hospitality manager
Hotel food services
Ice cream taster
Kitchen designer
Maître d'
Master chef
Menu designer
Molecular gastronomist
Mom and pop
Nutrition and dietetic technician
Nutrition educator
Nutrition services manager
Nutritionist
Pastry artist
Pastry chef
Personal chef
Prep cook
Private plane chef
Product developer
Public health worker
Recipe developer
Recipe taster
Recipe writer
Research chef
Restaurant designer
Restaurant manager
Restaurant owner
Short order cook
Sommelier

Sous chef
Tea shop owner
Urban farmer
Vegan chef

Waitstaff
Weight management professional
Winemaking

GOVERNMENT

Administrator of the EPA
Agricultural inspectors
Appraisers of real estate
Assessors
Assistant to the President
Campaign manager
Case manager
Case worker
Chief of Staff
CIA Director
City manager
Communications coordinator
Congressional aide
Congressman
Construction and building inspectors
Coroners
Counselor to the President
Deputy Assistant Inspector General
DC of Staff for Communications
Director of National Intelligence
Dir Office of Management & Budget
DNC internship
Financial examiners
Foreign service officer
Freight and cargo inspectors
GOP internship
Head of Securities and Exchange

Head of the Small Business Admin
House of Representatives
Inspector General
Intern/volunteer
Judge
Law clerk
Lawmakers
Legislative aide
Lobbyist
Mayor
Media strategist
National Security Advisor
Occupational Heath & Safety Spec.
Paralegal
Policy analyst
Political assistant
Political consultant
Political journalist
Political strategist
Pollster
Postal service
Press secretary
Regional political director
Revenue agents
Secretary of Agriculture
Secretary of Commerce
Secretary of Defense

Secretary of Education
Secretary of Energy
Secretary of Health & Human Svcs.
Secretary of Homeland Security
Secretary of Housing & Urban Devt.
Secretary of Labor
Secretary of State
Secretary of the Interior
Secretary of the Treasury
Secretary of Transportation
Secretary of Veteran Affairs
Senator
Senatorial aid
Senior Adviser to the President

Social media director
Socialist
Statistical assistants
Tax collectors
Tax examiners
Transportation inspectors
U.S. Ambassador to the UN
United States Attorney General
United States Diplomat
United States President
United States Trade Representative
United States Vice President
Urban and Regional Planners
WH National Economic Council Dir.

HEALTH/PERSONAL CARE

Aesthetician
Aromatherapist
Artificial tanner
Barber
Beautician
Beauty advisor
Beauty blogger
Beauty care blogger
Beauty care magazine writer
Beauty consultant
Beauty magazine
Beauty model
Beauty pageant director
Beauty school instructor
Beauty school owner
Beauty shop
Beauty store sales associate

Beauty technologist
Beauty therapist
Body piercer
Bodywork therapist
Color consultant
Colorist
Cosmetic surgeon
Cosmetic wig maker
Cosmetologist
Cosmetology
Cosmetology instructor
Cruise ship massage therapist
Cruise ship personal care specialist
Cruise ship personal trainer
Dermatologist
Direct sales beauty products
Electrologist

Esthetician

Fashion and wardrobe consultant

Fashion designer

Fashion model

Foot masseuse

Freelancer

Graphic design

Hair stylist

Hand model

Health and beauty therapist

Herbal beauty treatment specialist

Image consultant

Makeup artist

Manicurist

Marketing, sales and service

Massage therapist

Mobile masseuse

Mortuary beautician

Nail artist

Nail tech

Online beauty retailer

Pedicures

Pedicurist

Personal trainer gym

Product consultant

Recreation and fitness worker

Reflexologist

Salon manager

Skin care consultant

Skin care salon

Skin care specialist

Social media platforms

Somatologist

Specialty artist

Tattoo artist

Tattoo removal

Vitamin sales

Web merchandiser

Wellness and beauty

Wig retailer

HEALTHCARE

Behavioral disorder counselor

C-T technologist

Cardiologist

Cardiovascular

Cardiovascular lab tech

Case manager RN

Certified nursing assistant

Chaplain

Child psychologist

Chiropractor

Clinical dietician

Counselor

Couplet care

Cytology staff member

Dental assistant

Dental hygienist

Dentist

Doctor of osteopathy

Endocrinologist

Endoscopy tech

Float RN

Food service worker

Gynecologist
Histotechnologist
Home health
Hospice
Hospital cafeteria
Hospitalist physician
Hypno-therapist
ICU RN
Intern
Internist
IVF/fertility
Joint specialists
Licensed practical nurse
Marriage and family therapist
Maternal child clinical educator
Med tech
Medical assistant
Music therapy specialist
Neonatal RN
Neurologist
Newborn nursery assistant
Nurse practitioner
Nurse tech
Nursery RN
Occupational therapist
Oncologist
Operating room RN
Optometrist

Orthodontist
Pathologist
Patient transport
Pediatrician
Pharmacist
Pharmacy tech
Phlebotomist
Physical therapist
Physician's assistant
Podiatrist
Prosthetist
Prosthodontist
Psychiatrist
Psychologist
Radiation therapist
Radiologic technician
Registered nurse
Rehabilitation
Respiratory therapist
Social worker
Speech and language pathologist
Sterile processing specialist
Substance abuse counselor
Surgical tech
Therapist
Thoracic surgeon
Ultrasonographer

LAW ENFORCEMENT

Animal control
Arson investigator
ATF investigator

ATF special agent
ATF technician
Blood spatter analyst

CIA analyst

CIA special agent

Coast Guard

Computer forensics

Computer forensics investigator

Corrections officer

Counter terrorism

Crime laboratory analyst

Crime laboratory technician

Crime scene investigator

Criminal analyst

Criminal investigator

Criminalist

Criminologist

Crossing guard

Customs agent

DEA special agent

Dept. of Defense police officer

Deportation officer

Deputy U.S. Marshal

Deputy sheriff

Detective

Diplomatic security

EPA agent

ERO agent

Evidence technician

FBI special agent

Federal Air Marshal

Federal Protective Service

Fire inspector

Fire investigator

Fish & Game warden

Forensic accountant

Forensic ballistic expert

Forensic nurse

Forensic pathologist

Forensic psychologist

Forensic scientist

Forestry services

Fraud investigator

Gaming investigator

Gaming surveillance officers

Handwriting examiner

Homeland Security

Homicide detective

ICE special agent

Immigration inspector

Indian Affairs Office of Law ENF

Information security analyst

INS special agent

Intelligence analyst

IRS special agent

Juvenile probation counselor

Juvenile probation officer

K9 handler

K9 officer

K9 trainer

Narcotics officer

Naval Criminal Investigative agent

NSA officer

Parking enforcement officer

Penologist

Police dispatcher

Police officer

Prison warden

Probation officer

Protective service

Psychological profiler

Secret Service agent
Security guard
Sheriff
Ski patrol
Special agent
State trooper
Transit and railroad police
Forensic anthropologist

TSA screener
U.S. Border Patrol agent
U.S. Marshal
U.S. Park police
Uniformed Secret Service police
Victims advocate
Youth correctional counselor

LEGAL

Accident reconstructionist
Background investigator
Bailiff
Bankruptcy attorney
Broadcast captioner
Case manager
Chief court clerk
Child legal support attorney
Civil rights attorney
Compliance specialist
Computer forensics professional
Contract administrator
Contract attorney
Contract manager
Court clerk
Court interpreter
Court messenger
Court reporter
Courtroom deputy
Criminal attorney
Criminal defense
Criminal defense assistant
Criminal law paralegal

Defense attorney
Deputy court clerk
Divorce attorney
Document coder
Document delivery/process server
Document researcher
Electronic discovery professional
Entertainment attorney
Environmental attorney
Environmental law
Field investigator
File clerk
Forensic scientist
Immigration attorncy
Intellectual property lawyer
Investigations analyst
Judge
Judicial case processor
Judicial law clerk
Jury clerk
Jury consultant
Labor law
Law firm administrator

Law librarian
Legal analyst
Legal assistant
Legal document reviewer
Legal fellow
Legal intern
Legal secretary
Legal transcriptionist
Legal videographer
Litigation support professional
Litigator
Magistrate
Marshal

Mediator
Medical examiner
Paralegal
Personal injury attorney
Prosecutor
Public defender
Real estate attorney
Records clerk
Solicitor
Tax attorney
Technology product specialist
Trial consultant

MEDIA

Animator
Art Director
Assistant director
Assistant news director
Blogger
Breaking news editor
Broadcast network engineer
Broadcast news
Broadcast technician
Camera operator
Closed captionist
Columnist
Content producer
Content strategist
Copywriter
Director
Editor
Editorial columnist

Feature editor
Feature producer
Feature reporter
Film/video editor
Illustrator
Journalist
Lighting
Lighting technician
Lighting/compositing supervisor
Manga
News anchor
News director
News intern
News reporter
News talent coordinator
Newscaster
Photographer
Producer

Producer, nightly news
Production manager
Program manager
Public relations specialist
Radio announcer
Radio personality
Reporter
Segment producer
Social media specialist
Society columnist
Sound engineer
Sports news reporter
Sports news writer
Technical writer
Video games
Video producer
Visual development artist
Writer child picture books
Writer children/middle grade
Writer cowboy romance

Writer cozy mystery
Writer erotic romance
Writer erotica
Writer fantasy
Writer horror
Writer humor
Writer literary fiction
Writer mystery
Writer New Age/metaphysical
Writer non-fiction
Writer paranormal romance
Writer romance
Writer romantic suspense
Writer science fiction
Writer short story
Writer suspense/thriller
Writer westerns
Writer women's fiction
Writer young adult

PROFESSIONAL/OFFICE

Account manager
Accounting clerk
Administrative services manager
Advertising sales agent
Answering service
Assistant director
Auditing clerk
Auditor
Bank teller
Banker
Bill collector

Billing clerk
Bookkeeper
Brokerage clerk
Budget analyst
Call center
Chief executive officer
Chief financial officer
Chief technology officer
Clerical
Client relations manager
Computer programmer

Chief operating officer
Courier
Credit analyst
Customer service rep
Data entry operator
Database administrator
Director
Drafting and design technician
Executive assistant
Executive secretary
Facility manager
File clerk
Financial analyst
Financial clerk
Fraud investigator
General manager
General office clerk
Human resources administrator
Human resources coordinator
Insurance agent
Insurance appraiser
Insurance claims clerk
Insurance underwriter
Janitor
Mail clerk
Manager
Marketing
Marketing associate
Network systems analyst
Novelist
Office admin assistant
Office clerk
Online marketing analyst

Order filler
Personnel trainer
Positions
Postal clerk
Postmaster
President
Product management
Program administrator
Program director
Program manager
Programs coordinator
Project manager
Promotions manager
Public relations manager
Purchasing agent
Receptionist
Sales representative
Scheduler
Scheduling coordinator
Secretary
Software engineer
Special events coordinator
Staff assistant
Stock clerk
Telemarketer
Typist
Vice president
Virtual assistant
Web developer
Information systems
Wholesale buyer
Word processor

PROFESSIONAL/OTHER

Aerospace engineer
Air traffic controller
Aircraft assembler
Architect
Architectural drafter
Assessor
Audio visual technician
Aviation inspector
Bathroom design
Building inspector
Buyer
Camera repairer
Chemical engineer
City planner
Civil drafter
Civil engineering
Claims adjustor
Clergy
Compliance officer
Computer hardware tech
Computer repairer
Computer software tech
Computer support specialist
CPA/accountant
Decorator
Design
Diamond worker
Dress maker
Economist
Electrical engineer
Engineer
Environmental engineer

Event planner
Fashion designer
Field engineer
Floral designer
Funeral attendant
Funeral director
Geological engineer
Graphic designer
Hat maker
Home remodel
House sitter
Housekeeper
Industrial engineer
Insurance salesman
Interior design
Jewelry appraiser
Kitchen design
Librarian
Library worker
Loan counselor
Loan specialists
Logistics
Marine architect
Mechanical engineer
Mining engineer
Motor vehicle inspector
Museum conservator
Occupational health safety tech.
Pastor
Personal care worker
Postal mail carrier
Priest

Public transportation inspector
Radar technician
Rental clerk
Safety engineer
Seamstress
Silversmith
Stockbroker

Surveyors
Tax examiner
Tax preparer
Translator
Urban planner
Usher

RETAIL

Bed & bath stores
Big box stores
Bookstore
Bra fitter
Cashier
Commercial designer
Convenience store
Cosmetics
Department store
Fast food
Gas station
Hardware

Home Depot type stores
Industrial designer
Lumber store
Men's clothing
Paint supply store
Pool supply
Sales
Shoe salesman
Supermarket
Toy store
Walmart/Target type
Women's clothing

SCIENCES

Anthropologist
Archeologist
Astronomist
Atmospheric and space scientist
Biological scientist
Biologist
Chemicals
Chemist
Clinical laboratory technician

Conservation scientist
Entomologist
Environmental scientist
Geologist
Geoscientist
Mathematical scientist
Mathematician
Microbiologist
Physical scientist

Physicist

Sciences

Scientists

Wildlife biologist

Zoologists

SMALL BUSINESS OWNERS

Academic courses

Academy

Air conditioning/heater service

Alterations service

Antique refurbishing

Antique sales

App designer

Appliance repair

Architect

Audiobook producer

Auto repair

Baker

Bakery

Bar

Bath and body products

Bee farmer

Bicycle repair

Blogger

Boat charter

Boat tours

Bookkeeping and accounting

Business plan expert

Cake making

Campground

Candle maker

Canning products

Car detailing service

Carpet/upholstery cleaning

Carpet installer

Car resale

Car wash

Ceramics/pottery shop

Childcare service

Chimney sweep

Clothing alterations

Clothing retailer

Clown service

Coach

Coffee cart operator

Coffee shop

Collectibles

Compost sales

Computer repair

Computer setup and training

Consignment

Consulting

Cooking classes

Copywriting

Courier

Craft brewing

Dairy farm

Dance instructor

Day trader

Delivery service

Dessert shop

Distillery

Dog grooming

Dog walker

eBay seller

eBook author

eBook author services

eCommerce seller for eBay, Etsy, etc.

Editor

Electronics repair

eMagazine

Equipment rentals

Errand service

Estate sales

Event planner

Event venue

Fair food vendor

Farmer

Firewood sales

Fish farm

Flea market vendor

Florist

Food delivery

Food reviewer

Food truck

Freelance services

Freelance writer

Furniture maker

Game store

Gardener

Ghostwriter

Gift baskets

Gift wrapping service

Golf instructor

Gourmet candy

Graphic design

Gutter cleaner

Gym owner

Hairdresser

Hair salon

Handyman services

Heavy equipment operator

Herb grower

Holiday decorating

Holiday shop

Home cleaning service

Home contractor

Home improvement equipment

Home inspection

Horse trainer

Hot air balloon rides

Housekeeper

House painter

Ice cream stand

Indie bookstore

Information technology support

Interior decorator

Internet cafe

Juice bar

Junk removal service

Landscaping

Language courses

Life coach

Livestock farm

Livestreaming service

Logo design

Makeup artist

Marketing copywriter

Massage therapist

Meal preparation service

Mediator
Messenger service
Metal sculpting
Metaphysical/New Age store
Mobile business
Moving company
Musician
Music teacher
Nail salon
Office supply
Online bookstore
Online courses
Online game
Online school
Organic foods/dairy
Organic grocer
Organic market
Outdoor activity guide
Outdoor adventures
Party planning service
Personal assistant
Personal shopper
Personal trainer
Personal wellness
Pest control
Pet groomer
Pet sitting
Phone repair
Photographer
Plant nursery
Podcaster
Pool cleaner
Portrait photography
Poultry farm

Produce farm
Proofreader
Publicity
Public relations
Public speaker
Radio station
Rancher
Recycling service
Referee
Research service
Restaurant
Restaurant reviewer
Resume service
Roadside produce stand
Robotics
Roof installation and repair
Rooftop garden
Rooftop restaurant
Santa Claus service
Scout
Scrapbook maker
Search engine optimization specialist
Shopping mall
Shuttle service
Sign advertising
Snow removal
Soap and lotion maker
Social media influencer
Social media manager
Social media personality
Spa
Sports bar
Sports equipment rentals
Sports instruction

Sports store
Stock photographer
Storage facility
Street performer
Swim instructor
T-shirt designer
Tasting room
Tech rentals
Tech support
Tiny home renting
Tiny home sales
Tour guide company
Tour operator
Towing service

Translator
Travel planning
Truck driver
Tutor
Vacation rentals
Virtual assistant
Voiceover acting
Web design
Window washing
Wine bar
Woodworking
Yard sales
Yoga instructor

SMALL BUSINESS DIRECT SALES/HOME PARTIES

Accessories
Aromatic oils
Art
Baking and cooking
Fashion
Gifts and crafts
Health and home care products
Health supplements
Home products and decor
Jewelry

Beauty and skin care
Books
Candles
Diet and fitness
Kitchen supplies
Knives
Painting and wine
Scrapbooking and keepsake
Toys and games

TRADES/LABOR/ETC.

Aircraft assembler
Aircraft body repairer
Aircraft cargo handling
Aircraft mechanic

Appliance repair
Arborist
Armored vehicle driver
Assembler

Auto body
Auto repairman
Automatic teller machine service
Bicycle repairer
Block mason
Boat builder
Boilermaker
Brick mason
Cabinet maker
Cable/satellite installation
Carpenter
Carpet cleaning
Carpet installer
Cement mason & concrete finisher
Commercial driver
Construction carpenter
Construction equipment operator
Construction worker
Contractor
Diesel mechanic
Drywall installer
Electric motor repair
Electrician
Equipment operator
Farmer
Gardener
Gas pump station operator
Heat/AC service mechanic
Heating/cooling tech
Heavy equipment mechanic
Heavy equipment operator
Highway maintenance
Home builder
Housekeeper

Janitorial
Landscaper
Locksmith
Locomotive engineer
Logging equipment operator
Logging worker
Machinist
Maid
Marine mechanic
Mason
Meat packer
Mechanical engineer
Metal worker
Meter reader
Miner
Motorboat mechanic
Motorcycle repair
Mover
Oil well driller
Packer
Painter
Parking lot attendant
Pest control worker
Pipe fitter
Plaster
Plumber
Pool builder
Pool cleaner
Power plant operator
Production worker
Railroad yard worker
Railyard engineer
Refrigeration mechanic
Roofers

Rotary drill operator
Sailor
Semiconductor tech
Septic tank servicer
Service station attendant
Ship builders
Ship captain
Ship engineer
Shipping and receiving clerk
Shipwright
Steel worker
Stringed instrument repair
Stone cutter
Stonemason
Streetcar operator
Structural steel worker
Stucco
Surveyor
Textile machine operator
Textile worker
Ticket agent

Tile installer
Tire changer
Tool and die maker
Tool operator
Tractor/trailer driver
Traffic technician
Train crew member
Transformer repair
Transportation inspector
Tree trimmer
Truck driver
Typesetter
Upholsterer
Vending machine servicer
Warehouse
Water pump specialist
Water well driller
Welder
Window framer
Woodworker

TRAVEL

Air marshal
Airline mechanic
Bellhop
Car rental clerk
Chauffeur
Concierge
Cruise ship director
Cruise ship employee
Customs inspector
Flight attendant

Hotel desk clerk
Hotel housekeeping
Hotel reservation desk agent
Housekeeper
Immigration inspector
Lodging manager
Lyft/Uber
Pilot commercial
Pilot helicopter
Pilot small plane

Reservations
Taxi driver
Travel agent

Travel clerk
Travel guide
TSA officers

U.S. ARMED FORCES AND BRANCHES

Air Defense Artillery
Air Force
Air Force Special Tactics
Armor
Army
Army Green Beret
Army Medical Specialist Corps
Army Night Stalker
Army Nurse Corps
Army Reserve
Aviation
Chaplain Corps
Chemical Corps
Coast Guard
Corps of Engineers
Dental Corps
Finance Corps

Infantry
Judge Advocate Generals Corps
Marine Corps
Marine MARSOC
Marine RECON
Medical Corps
Medical Service Corps
Military Intelligence Corps
Military Police Corps
Navy
Navy SEAL
Ordnance Corps
Paratroopers
Signal Corps
Special Forces
Transportation Corps
Veterinary Corps

RELIGION/SPIRITUAL AND CULTS

CATHOLICISM

Archbishop
Acolyte
Bishop
Cardinal
Chaplain

Deacon
Mother Superior
Nun
Pope
Priest

BAPTIST

Deacon
Elder
Minister

Pastor
Preacher

METHODIST

Bishop
Chaplain
Clergywoman
Deacon

Elder
Pastor
Pastoral Counselor

PROTESTANTISM

Deacon
Minister
Pastor

Preacher
Reverend

LUTHERANISM

Bishop

Priest

JUDAISM

Hazzan

Rabbi

ISLAM

Ayatollah
Imam
Mufti
Mullah
Qadi

Shintoism
Kannushi
Priest
Shrine maiden

MORMONISM

Bishop
Branch President
Deacon

Missionary
Stake Presidents

JEHOVAH'S WITNESSES

Baptized/unbaptized publishers
Elders
Governing body
Ministerial servants

The students and associates
The Congregations
Traveling overseers

HINDUISM

Brahmin priest
Brahmin teacher

Gurus

SHINTOISM

Kannushi
Priest

Shrine maiden

PAGANISM

Arch Priest
High Priest
High Priestess
Lady

Lord
Priest
Priestess

SATANISM

Active Member
Maga/Magus

Magistra/Magister
Priestess/Priest

Registered Member   Witch/Warlock

ATHEISM/AGNOSTICISM

Generally a practice or belief, not formal spiritual organizations or religions

CULTS—ONLY A SMALL FRACTION OF CULTS

Astara
Christian Identity Movement
Christian Science
Falun Gong—China
Krishna
Native Ukrainian National Faith
Silva Mind Control
The Church of Scientology

The Family
The Farm
The Nation of Islam
The Twelve Tribes
Unification Church
United Church of America
Unity Church
Universal White Brotherhood

CHARACTER TRAITS

Creating great characters is an all-important aspect of story writing. Characters drive a good story, make us want to know, feel, and experience everything that is happening. Without characters, there is no story, so we need to create protagonists that readers can identify and sympathize with, and create antagonists the reader hates, but perhaps understands as well.

When we create a protagonist, we want to show the character's strengths but also weaknesses. Flaws are what make them "human," a character we can better relate to. Our heroine or hero may be an excellent martial artist with laser focus, but perhaps in the character's personal life he or she is distracted and forgetful. Readers don't want perfect characters. Flaws and failings make them real and better able to walk right off the page. Avoid clichés by choosing conflicting traits. Make your character your own, but one we want to read more about.

When it comes to antagonists, avoid complete clichés. Our villain needs more than an insidious laugh (Bwahahahaha!) and an evil grin. Our villain needs a backstory and something that makes the antagonist more human. The character could be cold, heartless, and ruthless when it comes to business, but might have a soft spot for kittens and supports a local cat shelter. The character may have a sick father in an assisted living center, visits him regularly and brings him lollipops. Remember too that villains don't see themselves as villains. They believe they are the heroes of their own stories.

In this section, we provide you with ideas for personality traits like quirks, phobias, obsessions, superstitions, and bad habits. We give you physical traits as well, where you can find ideas you might not have thought about for a character's appearance. When you create your character biography, you'll want to choose traits and other aspects that help define him or her.

Another important part of creating a character is naming. In *WSW*, we give you unusual male and female first names. When you find one you like, do a quick Internet search to check out the meaning behind the name to see if you feel it works for the character you are creating. Or, you might prefer a more common name and choose something familiar. Check out the meaning of whatever you like, and consider the decade or century you are placing your character in. Names mean a lot—you might want an antagonist with a strong name, but Rudolph doesn't quite give your hero the image you are looking for. Or you might want to choose Rudolph for a villain, and he hates the name and kills anyone who makes fun of him and asks him where his red nose is. You can make it comedic or evil. Take all the factors you want in a character and choose a name that fits whatever you are looking for.

Characters mean everything, so make sure you make yours memorable. Here are some ideas that might trigger your own ideas that will help you create strong characters.

PERSONALITY TRAITS

QUIRKS

Able to calculate complicated math in head
Acts helpless or dumb to attract men
Always asking for change
Always changing nail polish or getting nails done
Always losing reading glasses
Always playing games on iPad
Angry all the time
Asks a person weight or age
Asks questions twice
Articulates every word
Bad breath
Believes conspiracy theories
Bounces on toes when waiting
Buys new shoes frequently but doesn't wear them
Can never make up mind
Can't stand to listen to people smack, crunch, or chew gum
Carries a backpack everywhere
Carries a pillow when traveling
Carries deck of tarot cards everywhere but doesn't use them
Changing hairstyles constantly
Checks appearance in every mirror
Checks teeth in mirror
Checks watch constantly
Chews on nails
Cleans everything with bleach
Clears throat all the time
Coffee addict

Compulsive liar
Compulsively shops online
Constantly doodling
Constantly moving, can't stand still
Constantly sniffling
Continuously listening to music with earplugs
Crunches ice
Curses every other word
Dances to silent music
Daydreams constantly
Desk or room has to be ordered in a particular way
Difficulty walking in high heels
Does not clip toe or fingernails often
Drags feet while walking
Drives around corners too fast
Drums fingers
Eats BLTs every Thursday
Eats breakfast in the nude
Falls asleep on the couch instead of bed
Fiddles with earrings or ring
Fixes everything with duct tape
Forgetting something before leaving
Forgets everything
Gets a pedicure weekly
Goes to bed with the television on
Has ADHD
Has body odor
Has glaring phobia
Has OCD
Has to hold phone at all times
Hears voices or sounds no one else can
Hits the car remote twice to make sure it's locked
Hoards electronics from the 50s on
Hoards money and buries it in shoeboxes

Impatient in lines and in traffic

Keeps credit cards in cell phone case

Kicks off shoes somewhere in house and always forgets where

Kissing/touching partner in public places

Late to work all the time

Listens to classical music in car

Looks at phone to check the time while in conversation

Loves drama and creates it wherever she goes

Lying about her age

Mouth breather

Needs a fan while sleeping

Never carries a wallet while dining out with others

Never leaves work late

Never looks a person in the eyes

Never ties shoes

News junky

Nudging people on the shoulder

Obscene jokes

Only eats certain types of foods

Only eats or drinks certain colors of food—purple/white

Only shops at garage sales and flea markets

Only swims a certain stroke like the doggy paddle

Overly reacts on seeing certain animals or insects

Overthinks every situation

Passes gas all the time and never admits to it

Peels skin around nails

Picks at food and never really eats in public

Picks nose in public

Picks sores on face

Plays air guitar

Plays with ponytail while talking

Pops gum while talking

Pours orange juice over cornflakes for breakfast

Puts finger on end of nose while thinking

Puts on makeup while driving
Reading the same book again and again
Recites movie lines all the time
Refers to self in third person
Refuses to wear designer clothes
Relationships never last beyond a year
Repeats Biblical verses in awkward moments
Rocks side-to-side while talking
Rubs nose constantly
Scratching self all the time
Shuffles feet while talking
Sings in the shower
Sings while driving
Slurps soup
Smokes
Snores while sleeping
Squeezes a stress ball everywhere
Stares out into space frequently
Still uses nightlight as an adult
Stutters when nervous
Sweats easily
Takes selfies everywhere
Talks about cat or dog all the time
Talks as if each sentence is a question
Talks in a monotone
Talks to animals in a baby voice
Talks to self out loud
Talks to inanimate objects
Talks too loudly
Talks too softly
Talks with hands
Taps long fingernails while speaking
Types in all CAPS
Technology challenged

Texts at the dinner table
Ties a cherry stem with tongue
Touches chin with spoon before eating soup
Touching everyone else's hair to fix it
Tries to hide drinking but always has slurred speech
Tries to match-make with everyone
Twirls hair
Twists ring when nervous
Unable to be alone for any length of time
Uses acronyms all the time while talking
Using a toothpick or picks teeth
Very smart with computers
Walking ahead of everyone
Watches film noir on Wednesdays
Watches QVC all day
Wears clothing that is too large
Wears clothing that is too small
Wears only T-shirts and boxers at home even if company stops by
Wears striped socks when wearing sandals
Wears too much jewelry
Wears too much perfume
Wears unmatched socks
Wiggles toes at people
Will only wear clothes from Neiman Marcus
Will use credit card to have the best   Working long hours
of everything

NEGATIVE PERSONALITY TRAITS

Afraid

Aggressive

Aimless

Alcoholic

Angry

Anxious

Apathetic

Apprehensive

Argumentative

Arrogant

Audacious
Avoidant
Belligerent
Bigot
Blocking
Blunderer
Blunt
Boastful
Bold
Bored
Bossy
Brutal
Callous
Careless
Charmless
Childish
Clumsy
Complex
Conceited
Cowardly
Critical
Cruel
Cursed
Cynical
Dangerous
Deceitful
Dependent
Deranged
Destructive
Devious
Difficult
Discouraging
Discourteous
Dishonest

Disloyal
Disobedient
Disorderly
Disorganized
Disrespectful
Disruptive
Disturbed
Dyslexic
Egotistical
Envious
Erratic
Excessive guilt
Excessive selflessness
Faithless
Fanatical
Fearful
Feeling inferior
Feeling superior
Fickle
Fierce
Finicky
Fixated
Flirt
Foolish
Forgetful
Frightening
Frivolous
Giving into despair
Gloomy
Gluttonous
Greedy
Grim
Gruff
Gullible

Habitual	Lazy
Hard	Leniency to a fault
Hateful	Lewd
Haughty	Liar
Hedonistic	Loudmouth
Holding grudges	Low self-confidence
Hostile	Low self-esteem
Humorless	Lustful
Hypocritical	Machiavellianism
Hysterical	Martyr
Idiotic	Masochist
Ignorant	Mean
Illiterate	Meddlesome
Immature	Meek
Immoral	Megalomaniac
Impatient	Messy
Impractical	Misanthropy
Impulsive	Miserable
Incompetent	Monstrous
Inconsiderate	Moody
Indecisive	Naive
Indifferent	Narcissistic
Inept	Negative
Infamy	Neglectful
Insane	Nervous
Insincere	Nosey
Insolent	Obnoxious
Insulting	Obsession with neatness
Intolerant	Obsession with order
Irresponsible	Obsession with someone
Irritable	Obsessive
Jealous	Overambitious
Judgmental	Overconfident
Kleptomaniac	Overemotional

Overprotective

Overzealous

Paranoid

Passiveness

Peevish

Perfectionist

Pessimist

Petty

Politeness to a fault

Poor hygiene

Possessive

Power-hungry

Prejudiced

Promiscuous

Proud

Rebellious

Reckless

Reclusive

Refusing to forgive

Religious fanaticism

Remorseless

Resentful

Rude

Sadist

Sadomasochist

Sarcastic

Scornful

Sceptic

Secretive

Seducer

Self-indulgence

Self-righteous

Self-serving phoniness

Selfish

Senile

Shallow

Short-sighted

Shy

Sleazy

Sloppy

Sneaky

Snobbish

Solemn

Spineless

Spiteful

Spoiled

Stubborn

Superstitious

Tactless

Theatrical

Thoughtless

Timid

Tongue-tied

Too idealistic

Treacherous

Troublemaker

Unappreciative

Uncaring

Uncompromising

Uncooperative

Unforgiving

Unfriendly

Ungrateful

Unhealthy

Unlucky

Unpredictable

Unreliable

Untrustworthy

Vain
Vengeful
Violent
Weak
Weak-willed

Wicked
Withdrawn
Workaholic
Zealous

POSITIVE PERSONALITY TRAITS

Active
Admirable
Adventurous
Agreeable
Amiable
Amusing
Appreciative
Athletic
Authentic
Benevolent
Brave
Bright
Brilliant
Calm
Capable
Caring
Charming
Cheerful
Clean
Clear-headed
Clever
Compassionate
Confident
Considerate
Cooperative
Courageous

Courteous
Creative
Curious
Dedicated
Easygoing
Educated
Enthusiastic
Ethical
Exciting
Extraordinary
Fair
Firm
Focused
Forgiving
Friendly
Generous
Gentle
Good-natured
Grateful
Happy
Hardworking
Helpful
Heroic
Honest
Hopeful
Humble

Innocent

Intelligent

Inventive

Joyful

Kind

Lively

Loving

Loyal

Neat

Nice

Optimistic

Organized

Passionate

Patient

Peaceful

Playful

Polite

Principled

Reliable

Respectful

Responsible

Self-disciplined

Selfless

Sincere

Skillful

Strong

Sweet

Thoughtful

Trustworthy

Understanding

Unselfish

Wise

PHOBIAS/OBSESSIONS

Achievemephobia—fear of success

Acrophobia—fear of heights

Aerophobia—fear of flying

Agliophobia—fear of pain

Agoraphobia—fear of open and crowded places

Ailurophobe's—fear of cats

Androphobia—fear of men

Anthrophobia—fear of society

Apiphobia—fear of bees

Aquaphobia—fear of water

Arachnophobia—fear of spiders

Astraphobia—fear of thunder and lightning

Astrophobia—fear of kissing

Autophobia—fear of loneliness

Atychiphobia—fear of failure

Bacteriophobia—fear of germs

Basiphobia—fear of falling

Carcinophobia—fear of cancer

Claustrophobia—fear of closed places

Coasterphobia—fear of roller coasters

Coitphobia—fear of intercourse

Compulsion—obsessive urge to act

Coulrophobia—fear of clowns

Cynophobia—fear of dogs

Dipsomania—craving for alcohol

Disposophobia—fear of getting rid of things

Egomania—preoccupation with own self

Emetophobia—fear of vomiting

Entomophobia—fear of bugs and insects

Ergophobia—fear of work

Euphoria—excess and unrealistic feelings of happiness

Gerascophobia—excessive fear of getting old

Glossophobia—fear of public speaking

Gymnophobia—fear of nakedness

Gynophobia—fear of women

Hagiophobia—fear of sacred things

Haptephobia—fear of being touched

Heliophobia—fear of sun exposure

Hypersexuality—excessive sexual desire

Hypochondria—obsessive fear of becoming ill

Katsaridaphobia—fear of cockroaches

Kinemortophobia—fear of zombies

Kleptomania—compulsive urge to steal

Megalomania—excessive desire to become wealthy or have power

Metathesiophobia—fear of change

Monophobia—fear of being alone

Myrmecophobia—fear of ants

Mythomania—compulsion to lie or exaggerate

Narcissism—self love

Necromania—excessive fear of dead bodies
Necrophobia—fear of the dead
Neophobia—fear of new ideas or things
Nosocomephobia—fear of hospitals
Nyctophobia—fear of darkness
Oedipus complex—excessive attachment to a parent
Ombrophobia—fear of rain
Ophidiophobia—the fear of snakes
Paranoia—delusions of being persecuted
Pediophobia—fear of dolls
Pedophilia—sexual feelings toward children
Philophobia—fear of love
Phobophobia—fear of phobias
Photophobia—excessive dislike of light
Pogonophobia—excessive dislike of beards
Pyromania—obsessive desire to set fire to things
Pyrophobia—fear of fire
Scelerophobia—fear of crime
Schizophrenia—delusions in escaping from reality
Somniphobia—fear of sleep
Taphephobia—fear of being buried alive
Thanatophobia—fear of death
Theophobia—fear of God
Tokophobia—fear of pregnancy
Traikaideaphobia—fear of the number 13
Vehophobia—fear of driving
Xenophobia—fear of strangers
Zoophobia—fear of animals

SUPERSTITIONS

A nut with two kernels is lucky; one nut should be eaten and the other given to a friend or tossed over the left shoulder while making a wish

A pimple on the tongue indicates the person is prone to lying

A white pigeon that settles on a rooftop is a sign of imminent death of someone inside

A woman not kissing under the mistletoe will risk dying unmarried

Bad luck comes in threes

Beginners luck

Blackbirds are a harbinger of death

Blowing out all the candles on birthday cake to make wish come true

Breaking a chopstick will bring bad luck

Breaking a glass vase by accident is a good omen and seven years of good luck

Breaking a mirror brings seven years bad luck

Breaking a wishbone is good luck if you get the larger side

Carrying a piece of coal is lucky

Crossing your fingers for good luck

Don't let a black cat cross your path

Don't open an umbrella inside

Don't walk under a ladder

Ears are burning means someone is talking about you

Eating whole chili peppers will stop a cold

Evil eye

Finding a horseshoe is good luck

Finding old hole-punched coins brings great luck

Fortune cookies can determine good luck or bad luck

Four-leaf clover brings good luck

Friday the 13th

Hanging a horseshoe over door brings good luck

Hemlock is associated with the devil

Holy water can drive out evil spirits and heal almost any ailment

If you spill salt, throw it over your left shoulder to ward off evil spirits

Itchy palm is a tell for greed

It is unlucky for engaged couples to have a photograph taken together and threatens chances of being married

Keep money only in one pocket

Knocking on wood for good luck

Leaving purse on floor or ground leads to financial problems

Making sign of cross to ward off evil

No 13th floor in buildings

Number 666 is considered the evilest of numbers and is thought to be the number of the Beast or the Devil

Number nine is considered very lucky and is the number of months between conception and birth

Number one is lucky and associated with God and the sun

Number seven is considered supernatural and will bring success to any project

Number thirteen is bad luck

Number thirteen is considered unlucky and began because Judas was the thirteenth disciple to sit at the last supper.

Number three is considered to have special powers because of the concept of the Trinity in Christianity

Opal considered the unluckiest stones and dangerous to own

Oysters are considered a strong aphrodisiac

Peacock feathers are unlucky and hold the evil eye

Picking up a penny brings good luck. Passing it brings bad luck

Rabbit's foot is a good luck charm

Saying "God bless you" when someone sneezes is good luck

Stepping on a crack will break your mother's back

Wishing at 11:11 will make your wish come true

A picture falling off a wall is a bad omen

PHYSICAL TRAITS

* Please note: Writing about a group or person's physical appearance and background should be done with respect. If in doubt, do your research. The following are a few resources. There are far more available on the Internet.

Writing the Other: https://www.amazon.com/Writing-Other-Conversation-Pieces-8/dp/193350000X/

Writing With Color: https://writingwithcolor.tumblr.com/

Ylva Publishing: https://www.ylva-publishing.com/2018/05/29/avoiding-racism-writing-coffee-honey-colors/

BODY

Anorexic—terribly thin to the point a person looks ill
Athletic—physically active and strong; good at sports
Barrel-chested—large, broad chest compared to rest of body
Beefy—large, dense, muscular body
Beer-bellied—large, fat, protruding stomach caused from drinking beer
Bent—stooped
Big-bellied—large, fat, prominent stomach
Big-boned—having large bones; large but not obese
Bony—skinny to the point where bones become prominent
Bosomy—have large breasts
Brawny—muscular, heavily built
Brittle—easily breakable; thin and fragile
Built—muscular; physically attractive with well-developed muscles
Bulky—excess body mass, especially muscle
Bull-necked—short, thick neck

Burly—muscular and heavily built

Buxom—curvy, having pleasing curves, looks healthy and attractive

Chubby—containing a moderate amount of fat

Chunky—dense and thick-bodied, sometimes muscular

Colossal—suggesting the stupendous in power or bulk

Coltish—slender with longer than average limbs

Compact—solid, without excess flesh

Corpulent—very fat or obese

Curvaceous—pleasing curves; well-proportioned figure

Curvy—large hips and breasts

Dainty—delicate

Deformed—misshapen, especially in body or limbs

Delicate—fragile or easily broken

Diminutive—petite

Dimpled—crease, in some soft part of body, particularly on a cheek

Doughy—soft and heavy or also flabby

Dumpy—fat; squat; thick in build

Elephantine—large like an elephant; enormous in build or strength

Emaciated—skeletal-looking, dangerously thin

Eye-catching—boldly attractive, striking

Fat—overly high body fat; lacking lean muscle; obese

Feeble—physically weak, frail, possibly from sickness

Flabby—lacking firmness with flesh

Fleshy—thick and plump; large person

Flimsy—weak or inadequate body

Fragile—vulnerable and lacking strength or substance

Full-figured—large frame; filled-out body

Gangly—all arms and legs; loose-jointed movement; tall and thin

Gargantuan—massive in size

Gaunt—very thin, particularly from an illness, haggard and drawn

Ginormous—extremely large, humongous

Gnarled—knotty and old; twisted joints

Goliath—tall, symbolic meaning of great, larger than life

Haggard—gaunt, exhausted, or wasted in appearance

Hale—hearty, filled with health and vigor
Hardy—great physical vigor, robust, able to withstand fatigue or hardship
Herculean—enormous strength, related to Hercules
Hunchbacked—back with large, round lump
Hunched—bowed back, or rounded shoulders and back
Husky—powerful, burly, muscles
Infirm—sickly, weak in body or health
Jaundiced—yellowed skin
Lanky—tall and thin, long slender limbs
Lavishly endowed—curvy, large breasted and full hips
Lean—low body fat
Leathery—skin like leather, tough and wrinkled
Leggy—long shapely legs; disproportionately long legs
Lethargic—fatigued, sleepy
Limber—agile, being flexible
Lissome—supple, flexible, and nimble
Lithe—flexible, even graceful, pliant
Loose-jointed—flexible at elbows, knees, and other joints
Lumpy—full of lumps, usually large; large bulges
Malnourished—bony, emaciated, skinny to point of being unhealthy
Mammoth—overly large
Massive—usually solid and large in size
Meaty—big and strong, broad, large and solid
Mesomorphic—greater than average muscle
Neckless—head joined to the shoulders and body; odd shape with no neck
Nimble—agile, quick, ease of movement
Obese—fat, overweight, excess body weight
Palsied—normal physical or mental function is impaired
Paunchy—large and protruding stomach
Pear-shaped—body weight allocated to thighs, hips & buttocks
Petite—short, small, fine-boned
Physical—strong, muscular, and capable
Pigeon-chested—protrusion of sternum and ribs from rest of body
Pliant—supple, adaptable, and flexible

Plump—chubby

Pocket-sized—small and petite

Portly—bulky, overweight, and stout

Pot-bellied—large, protruding body, the shape of a cooking pot

Puny—weak, thin, and small

Rawboned—large-boned, large frame

Reed-like—slender, thin, resembling a reed or twig

Resilient—maintaining strength and stamina while challenged

Rickety—not stable, frail, and easily overbalanced

Ripped—very low percentage of body fat, high range of muscle mass

Robust—healthy, strong, and vigorous

Roly-poly—shaped like a ball, fat, and round

Ropy—slender but strong, sinewy

Rotund—round and plump

Rugged—sturdy and strong

Scrawny—thin and meager in body

Serpentine—flexible, slender, and curved like a snake

Shapeless—no physical form, lacking curves or muscle

Short-waisted—lacking a normal waist length or curve between hip & breast

Shrunken—physically haggard, smaller than before, frail

Sickly—unhealthy, lacking physical strength or energy

Sinewy—muscular, strong muscles but lacking fat

Skeletal—bones appearing against the skin, little flesh or muscle

Sleek—well-groomed, smooth, and streamlined

Slender—long, thin, and graceful in an attractive way

Slight—slender, not heavy

Slim—thin and slender, lacking bulk

Slinky—sexy, seductive

Slouched—stooped head and shoulders

Spidery—thin, narrow, slow movement

Spindly—usually related to limbs, long and lean, suggest physical weakness

Squat—short and thick

Stacked—full-breasted with attractive curves

Stalwart—outstanding strength, hardy and robust

Starved—skinny, thin, as if have not eaten for days
Stately—lofty, impressive in size
Statuesque—a tall person, having poise and grace
Stocky—heavy and compact
Stooped—bent upper body, hunched over
Stout—firm, tough or sturdy
Strapping—strong, vigorous, and sturdy
Svelte—appearance of refinement, graceful, moving with confidence & ease
Sylphlike—attractive, thin and supple
Symmetrical—perfectly proportioned, pleasing to the eye
Tall—height is above average
Thick-waisted—lacking hour-glass figure, waist not much thinner than hips
Thickset—thick body; stout
Thin—slender, slim
Top-heavy—large breasted
Towering—much taller than the norm
Tubby—large stomach, slightly fat
Vertically challenged—petite
Voluptuous—curvy, easily in the chest area
Waspish—slender waist, wasp-like appearance
Weak—fragile
Wee—petite
Weedy—slender, pliant, worn-out
Well-endowed—full-breasted, curvy
Well-muscled—lacking body fat, well-developed muscles
Well-padded—extra weight or fat
Whip-thin—very slender or thin, appearing as skinny as a whip
Willowy—flexible and graceful
Wimpy—lacking strength
Wiry—sinewy, lean, and strong
Withered—thin, shriveled
Wizened—old and worn-out
Wooden—lacking agility, expression, or smooth movement
Youthful—limber, agile, looking young, young appearance

CHEEKS

Angular—prominent cheekbones
Chubby—chunky or fat
Dimpled—dimples on either side of mouth
Drawn—lacking flesh
Flabby—loose and fat
Freckled—small, pale brown spots on the skin
Hollow—indentations below the cheekbone
Jowly—loose skin as if having pouches on either side
Pendulous—loose skin on either side of mouth
Puffy—rounded and full
Rosy—flushed and pink
Saggy—loose skin that hangs
Sunken—shadows/indentations beneath cheekbones

EYES

Almond—shaped like the almond
Avid—interested, enthusiastic
Beady—small and round
Bedroom—dreamy, amorous stare
Bleary—unfocused, tired, or reddened
Bloodshot—red, bloody, inflamed
Bright—clear
Bug—protruding
Bulging—protruding, large
Button—small round or large round, wide
Cat-like—almond shaped; shape like a cat's
Cataract—cloudy from buildup of protein
Close-set—eyes close together
Cloudy—sad, turbulent
Cock-eyed—both eyes looking in different directions
Crescent—shaped between a quarter and half moon

Cross-eyed—both eyes looking inward

Deep-set—prominent brow; eyes that are set farther into the skull

Doe-eyed—innocent

Dopey—unintelligent, droopy

Dull—lifeless, lacking brightness

Egg-shaped—large, shaped like an egg

Empty—no emotion

Expressive—showing emotion

Falcon—sharp, small, and round

Feline—cat-like

Flint-eyed—serious quality or manner

Fish-like—round, protruding and emotionless

Fringed—lashes circling the eye

Gimlet—piercing or penetrating

Glazed—unfocused, lack of concentration

Glittering—sparkling

Glass—an eye replacement

Glassy—shiny

Goggle—wide opened, at times in amazement

Hardened—cold or dispassionate in feeling

Heavy-lidded—large or thick lids

Hollow—deeply sunken eyes, without emotion

Hooded—layer of skin that droops over crease; hiding expression/thoughts

Jaundiced—yellowish tint to whites of the eyes from the condition

Knowing—shrewd, keenly alert

Livid—bright

Luminous—emitting or reflecting steady, suffused, or glowing light.

Languid—lacking energy or enthusiasm

Lively—bright and full of energy

Moody—dark with emotion

Mesmerizing—fascinating or interesting eyes

Owlish—large, unblinking, possibly eyes behind glasses that magnify

Oval—football shape

Pearly—white, mother of pearl shine

Pale—blanched
Pea—small and round
Protuberant—bulging
Rheumy—watery or moist
Saucer—large and round, staring
Slitted—narrow, thin; lowered eyelids where only sliver of eye appears
Sloe—almond shaped, dark, and large
Pie-eyed—intoxicated, possible dilated pupils
Sultry—suggesting passion
Squinty—narrowed, hard to see
Steely—filled with resolve, unbending
Sunken—hollowed out below brow
Twinkling—sparkling
Unfocused—glazed
Walleyed—large, glossy, fishlike
Wide-set—eyes set apart more than normal
Wood eye—false eye
Witchy—strange, filled with enjoyment
Weary—fatigued; tired
Wary—cautious

FACIAL HAIR

Anchor beard—short, pointed beard that traces the jawline
Assyrian beard—long beard with plaits or spirals
Balbo beard—trimmed beard without sideburns
Beard—any style of facial hair that isn't clean-shaven or just a mustache
Belgrave beard—neatly groomed mid-length beard
Boxed beard—short, neatly trimmed full beard alternative
Cadiz beard—mid-length pointed beard
Cathedral or French Fork beard—full beard split into two tails at the bottom
Chevron—mustache covering entire top lip/inverted V
Chin curtain—full beard without mustache or neck hair
Chin strip—small vertical line on chin

Chinstrap style beard—line of beard along edge of jaw/chin & no mustache
Circle beard—a chin patch of hair and a mustache that forms a circle
Ducktail beard—longer length beard trimmed to a tapered point
Fu Manchu—thin, narrow mustache that grows downward to pointed ends
Goatee—a goat-like beard/patch of hair at chin
Grizzly beard—gray, or flecked with gray beard
Gunslinger beard & mustache—flared sideburns with a horseshoe mustache
Handlebar mustache—long mustache with ends turned upward in a curl
Hebraic beard—long, full, and untrimmed beard
Horseshoe mustache—resembled a horseshoe pointed downward
Imperial beard—thick handlebar-like mustache with a long beard on chin
Mustache—facial hair grown above the upper lip
Mustache wax—pomade or gel to hold mustache hairs in place
Mutton chops beard—thick sideburns connecting to mustache/no chin hair
Neckbeard—hair on neck or under jaw but absent on face
Ned Kelly beard—full beard and mustache with short hair usually
Original stache—trimmed mustache sitting above the top lip
Peach fuzz—adolescent hair, not thick enough to shave yet
Pencil beard—very thin, pencil-like mustache above the upper lip
Petite goatee—small beard/patch at chin
Playoff beard—athletes not shaving beards during playoffs
Royale beard—a chin strip and a mustache separated by skin
Shenandoah—common in 19th century, full beard with trimmed mustache
Side whiskers—extreme sideburns and/or mutton chops
Sideburns—hair grown in front of ears but not extended into a beard
Soul patch—very small section of hair grown below the bottom lip
Stiletto beard—slender and long pointed beard
Super Mario—thick mustache shaped like a wide U
Terminal beard—beard grown until it can no longer grow further
The Zappa—full mustache extended downward, named after Frank Zappa
Three-day stubble beard—trimmed beard resembling three days of stubble
Toothbrush—shape similar to toothbrush above lip, worn by Adolf Hitler
Van Dyke beard—a goatee with a detached mustache
Walrus mustache—droops over mouth, resembles walrus whiskers

HAIR

Afro—short and very curly, forming a bowl-shaped profile

Ash blond—lacks red or gold highlights

Ash brown—brown color lacking warm/red tones

Asymmetric—cut long on side of the head and short on the other

Bangs—front of hair cut to fall and cover the forehead

Bedhead—short to mid-length shaggy cut, usually moussed

Beehive—hair piled on top of head toward back to resemble a beehive

Bird's nest—unruly, matted

Bob—introduced in 1915, short cropped hairstyle, popular during 1920's

Bouffant—backcombed or ratted hair, smoothed into a bubble appearance

Bowl—bowl line around the head.

Braided—can be single or more braids

Brassy—an almost metallic sheen to hair

Bubble—60's hairstyle, backcombed to appear like bubble around head

Bun—pulled back from face, twisted/plaited, and a circular coil around itself

Bushy—thick, full, usually close to head

Buzz—shaved close to the head

Chignon—a roll/knot of hair swept to the back of the head or the nape

Coiffure—a style of arranging or combing the hair

Coiled—hair continuously wound and spaced rings one above the other

Combed—neat and tidy

Comb over—hair combed over top of bald spot from side

Cornrows—small tightly braided rows of hair close to the scalp

Coarse—opposite of thin or smooth

Crimping—usually straight hair styled often in a sawtooth or zig-zag fashion

Crewcut/GI—short, stands on end at front of head, shaved on sides

Curls—light or tight curves and spirals

Downy—very soft, like the feathers of a baby duck or chicken

Dreadlock—ropelike strands of hair formed by matting or braiding hair

Ebony—very dark or black hair

Expresso—very dark brown hair

Fair-haired— light-colored

Fine— hair in which the diameter of each individual strand is thin

Fluffy—soft and light

Flyaway—loose strands of hair, usually soft and light to the touch

Frazzled—damaged, unkept or frizzy

Fringe—strands long enough to fall over the forehead but above the eyes

Frizzy—curled tightly, damaged

Fuzzy—very short, like a peach coating; tightly curled

Greasy—oily

Grizzled—sprinkled or streaked with gray, also coarse hair

Kinky—tight curls

Kiss curls—curls/ringlets against the cheeks or face; popular after Civil War

Knotted—matted

Limp—lifeless, has no volume

Lock/locks—a piece or pieces of hair

Lustrous—shiny and brilliant

Mahogany—dark brown with a red tint

Man bun—male with partial bun or full bun on top or back of head

Mane—long, thick hair

Matted—knotted and tangled

Mohawk—shaved on both sides of the head with strip of long hair in center

Mop—thick mass of hair, like a mop

Oily—greasy; grease build-up

Pageboy—straight hair below the ear, usually turns under and has bangs

Pig-tailed—hair is parted down middle and each side is tied into a ponytail

Pixie—short cut; feathered; usually full bang and combed forward

Plaited—braided

Platinum-blond—pale silvery-blond

Pompadour— hair high over the forehead usually with a rolled effect

Ponytail—hair pulled and tied together to make a tail at the back of the head

Poodle cut—style with short, tight curls

Powdered hair/wigs—worn late 1700s to early 1800s

Punk—twist on popular haircut, mohawk with spikes, neon/rainbow colors

Raven—black hair with a blue sheen

Redhead—red hair

Ringlets—tube or corkscrew curls

Sausage curl—a lock of hair formed into a curl resembling a sausage in shape

Scraggly—ragged and unkempt

Shaggy—long and in need of a hair cut

Shaven—cut close to the scalp, can be to the point of being bald

Shock—mass of bushy hair

Shorn—cut or clipped

Silver—predominantly white hair, brighter and shinier than gray

Skinhead—radical racist youths who have a shaved head

Slicked—treated with hair gel and combed straight back/greasy

Straight—without curl

Strands—individual lengths of hair

Stringy—fine and oily/lifeless

Stubbly—unshaven/day or two growth to beard or hair after being shaved

Tangled—knotted, jumbled strands

Tonsure—monk/cleric's hair cut short or shaved as a bald patch on top

Towhead—whitish blond hair

Tresses—long unbound hair

Tufts—small clusters of outgrowths or parts attached to scalp

Updo/upsweep—long hair styled high on top of head

Warm blond—blond with a hint of gold and red

Wavy—loose curls

Wedge cut—retro-style short layered bob

Wig—synthetic or real hair that covers all or most of the head

Wild—unkempt, untamable

Wiry—stiff and wild hair

Woven—plaited or braided

JAW

Angular—prominent chin with sharp edges

Heavy jaw—large jaw that looks like it holds a lot of weight

Pointed chin—sharp angle that narrows at chin

Receding chin—lacks prominence

Round chin—circular curve
Slack-jawed—unable to close mouth
Cleft chin—dimple that separates chin into two
Double chin—two chins, one below the other; a pouch below chin
Square—the shape of the bottom of a square

MOUTH

Bee-stung—full and sultry
Bowed—resembling the bow of a cupid
Chapped—lined and dry
Cleft-lip—section of lip missing or draw upward
Collagen-filled—full, rounded, and thick
Cracked—lined deeply
Dour—turned down at the corners, aged and dry
Dry—lacking moisture
Fat—overly round and thick
Full—rounded and thick
Hair-lip—section of lip missing or draw upward
Misshapen—unusually shaped
Pallid—pale
Petulant—turned down at corners
Pierced—has a bar or metal circle ring in lip
Pinched—thin, narrow
Plump—thick and full
Pouty—full, lower lip protruding
Puckered—shaped as if about to kiss; twisted into a grimace
Rose petal—small with rounded shape
Scabby—covered with dry sores
Sultry—full, moist
Swollen—full and thick

NOSE

Beaked—hawkish like the bird
Bent—usually a broken nose
Broken—has a nasal bump or hump
Bulbous—large, rounded curved tip
Button—small circular
Chiseled—smooth, angular, rigid like stone
Concave—curves outward in the center
Convex—curves inward in the center
Flaring—nostrils are flared
Flat—bridge and tip are flat against the face
Fleshy—usually bulbous nose and a larger percentage of flesh
Gourd-like—unusual or misshapen, usually large
Grecian/Greek—straight, smooth, narrow nostrils
Hawk—beakish, prominent bridge
High-cut—nostrils are cut higher than normal
Hooked—curved at end, beaked
Pig-like—pressed toward face, flat, similar to a pig
Pug—like the dog, small and flat against the face but protruding at base
Roman—gentle slope to the nose, prominent against the face
Skewed—crooked
Snub—thin and subtle point at the tip, slightly rounder shape
Up-turned—protruding at the tip

COMPLEXION

Acne—pimples
Age spots—spotting from age
Alligator—scaly or very rough skin
Blemished—marks to skin, including pimples, sores, or scars
Blotchy—mottled, spotted, uneven skin tones
Cadaverous—colorless or corpse-like
Chapped—dry, lined, split, cracked and rough

Coarse—rough, not smooth
Cratered—pitted skin from acne or illness
Cyanotic—lack of oxygen turning skin to blue or gray
Dirty—covered in dirt
Dusty—covered in dust
Downy—soft and fine like chick feathers
Filthy—dirty
Flawless—without blemishes
Freckled—spotted
Greasy—oily
Jaundiced—yellow color to skin and eyes from illness
Leathery—thick textures skin, like leather
Lentigo—brownish spot but not a freckle
Livid—black or blue or grayish blue or lead-colored
Mottled—spotted or blotchy
Nevus—birthmark
Oily—greasy
Pitted—indented, deep small scarring
Pocked—scarring from smallpox, pitted
Pustules—pus oozing from sores
Raw—sore, red, inflamed
Sandpapered—rough, coarse
Scarred—damaged or disfigured
Shriveled—wrinkled, withered
Splotchy—spotted, mottled
Warty—raised bumps, many warts
Weather-beaten—wrinkled or leather-like from the outside elements
Weathered—wrinkles or like leather from sun and wind
Wizened—old and wrinkled or shriveled
Wrinkled—lined

TEETH

Abscessed—usually caused by bacterial infection
Baby—temporary tooth that is later replaced by permanent tooth
Buckteeth—upper teeth that project over the lower lip
Canine—like the teeth of a dog
Crooked—bent out of shape
Dazzling—extremely bright
Dentures—set of artificial teeth
Eroded—loss of tooth surface
Extracted—tooth removed from its socket in the bone
Fangs—large sharp teeth resembling a dog's incisors
Gap-toothed—spacing between teeth
Jagged—uneven edge
Needle-sharp—shaped like a needle and as sharp
Overcrowded—where the jaw is too small for the size of teeth
Pearly—white and lustrous
Permanent—teeth that replace baby teeth
Pitted—many small holes or dents
Pointy/pointed—end/tips that have sharp edges; point at one end
Predatory—teeth resembling carnivores
Razer-sharp—very sharp, similar to a razor
Rotten—decay of tooth, loss of enamel
Saw-toothed—alternate steep and gentle slopes; like the teeth of a saw
Serrated—ends like a serrated blade lined with small teeth
Snaggle-toothed—irregular, broken tooth, or projecting from the others
Stained—discoloration by food, drink or smoking
Tusks—greatly enlarged teeth that are elongated
Underbite—the lower teeth project over the top teeth; similar to a bulldog
Uneven—crooked, misshapen
Vampirish—like vampire teeth; large pointed tooth
Veneered—layer of material placed around the teeth
Well-kept—taken care of
Wooden—made from wood

CHARACTER NAMING

UNUSUAL FEMALE NAMES

A

Abella
Aberdeen
Abiela
Abilene
Abra
Adalyn
Adara
Addy
Adeja
Adilyn
Adonia
Adora
Adriele
Aeliana
Aerilyn
Afton
Ahna
Aidan
Aideen
Aila
Ainara
Aisha
Akasha

Akira
Alafair
Alameda
Alamira
Aliyah
Amaya
Amika
Amina
Amorina
Anah
Anistana
Aniyah
Aralyn

Ari
Ariadne
Asta
Astrea
Atlee
Aubrianna
Avari
Avelyn
Avi
Ayana
Ayla
Aysha
Azia

B

Babette
Badaidra
Bakari
Bala
Bali
Ballencia
Bardot
Basilia
Bastet
Bathsheba
Belen
Bellatrix
Bellerose
Bellissa
Benedetta
Benicia
Bentley
Berdine

Berkeley
Berlyn
Bernyce
Beryl
Bethel
Bey
Binah
Blakeley
Blysse
Blythe
Bohemia
Braelyn
Brennan
Brette
Brielle
Brienne
Briley
Brina

Brinkley
Brinley
Brionna
Briony
Bryanna
Bryce
Brylie

Bryna
Brynlee
Bryony
Brystol
Bryton
Byrne

C

Caaliyah
Caasi
Cachelle
Cadee
Cai
Calais
Callen
Camber
Cameo
Camisha
Camryn
Caoimhe
Caralynn
Carlena
Cassiopeia
Caylin
Ceaira
Ceana
Cebrina
Cecily
Ceejae
Ceinwyn
Celestia
Cersei
Cerys

Charla
Chenille
Cherris
Chevelle
Chrystal
Chynna
Ciana
Ciari
Cicely
Ciel
Cierra
Circe
Clancy
Clea
Cobee
Cocoro
Consuelo
Corin
Cressida
Cricket
Cuinn
Cyane
Cynna
Cyra

D

Daaimah
Daciana
Daedree
Daegen
Daelan
Daire
Dalee
Damaris
Danara
Dashiell
Daviana
Davina
Deaija
Decarria
Deccie
Delaney
Delphine
Demetria
Deniz
Devi
Devonn
Dharma
Diamondique
Diandra

Dieko
Diem
Dienelis
Dinorah
Dion
Dmitriana
Dolcie
Domenica
Dominica
Donatella
Donelle
Dorrin
Dory
Dresdyn
Dublyn
Dugan
Dulcie
Dustina
Dvorah
Dyamond
Dyani
Dylanne
Dylynn
Dzenana

E

Eada
Eaden
Eadlyn
Eartha
Eastan

Ebba
Echelle
Echoe
Effa
Ehla

Eiliana
Eilidh
Ekaterina
Electra
Elfrida
Elleana
Ellice
Ellorie
Elspeth
Elva
Emah
Ember
Emerelda
Emiko
EmRose
Ena
Enid
Enola
Eowyn
Ephie

Eranthe
Erista
Erlinda
Erna
Erynne
Esella
Esme
Espy
Essela
Etta
Eulalia
Evadne
Evanthe
Evelina
Evia
Evie
Eviris
Evolette
Ezmeray

F

Fabiane
Fabita
Fable
Fabriana
Fabrice
Fadra
Fae
Faelynn
Fahari
Fairlie
Fairlight

Faiza
Farlyn
Faron
Farren
Fawn
Fayla
Faylee
Fayola
Febbie
Feda
Fedora

Fenia

Fennel

Fennma

Fia

Fiana

Fidella

Fina

Finley

Finnegan

Finola

Fireese

Flannery

Flavia

Fleur

Flynn

Fogh

Folia

Fonisha

Forever

Fortuna

Freya

Fuchsia

Furne

Fyfe

Fynch

Fynleigh

Fyona

G

Gabi

Gabri

Gabrianna

Gacie

Gadea

Gaia

Galiena

Galilee

Galina

Garnet

Gaylyn

Geanah

Geanette

Gegee

Gehana

Gemma

Genavee

Genece

Geneen

Genesys

Geneva

Genevra

Genneta

Gert

Gia

Gigi

Ginevra

Giovanna

Giselle

Giulio

Glynda

Godavari

Godiva

Golda

Gordana
Govanna
Graceleigh
Gracia
Gracyn
Graylin
Greenlee
Greysen

Guen
Guianna
Gwenda
Gwinne
Gwyn
Gyllian
Gyviana

H

Habi
Habika
Hadalee
Haddison
Hadwyn
Haiku
Hannahlynn
Hannie
Hansen
Hansi
Hara
Haranya
Harlow
Harmonie
Hart
Healey
Heatherlynne
Heavynne
Heidynn
Hela
Helaena
Helyn
Henley

Hennie
Henrienna
Hera
Herlinda
Hester
Hialeah
Hiede
Hikari
Hilena
Himanya
Hiona
Hiyasha
Holleigh
Hollis
Honora
Honorata
Huai
Huberta
Hudson
Hulali
Humayrah
Hyacinth
Hyatt

Hyley
Hypatia

Hyzlan

I

Ialla
Ianthe
Ibby
Ida
Idabel
Idalah
Idalia
Idele
Idra
Idris
Ieesha
Ignacia
Ila
Iliana
Ilisa
Illyana
Ilsa
Ilyssa
Imani
Imogene
Inaaya
Inara
Inaya
Indigo
Indira

Ineka
Ira
Irelyn
Irie
Irina
Isabeau
Isadora
Ishanvi
Isis
Isobel
Isolde
Isolina
Isrielle
Itsuki
Itzayana
Iva
Ivee
Ivonne
Ivory
Ivyonna
Iyanna
Izabella
Izora
Izzy

J

Jacinda

Jaclynne

Jacoba
Jacobina
Jacquetta
Jacynthe
Jadira
Jadis
Jaedynne
Jael
Jahnavi
Jaimah
Jalaanea
Janaliz
Janiah
Janina
Javiera
Jaxine
Jayla
Jaylee
Jeanay
Jeanique
Jeena
Jemma
Jenae
Jenica

Jerelyn
Jessamy
Jessenia
Jetta
Jianne
Jinia
Jiya
Joaida
Jocasta
Jodelle
Johnet
Joie
Jonalyn
Jord
Julesa
Julina
Juliska
Julissa
Junifa
Juztina
Jyl
Jyllina
Jyoti

K

Kadienne
Kaelah
Kahli
Kailey
Kamala
Kanti
Kassiani

Kataleya
Kaydence
Kazuko
Kazumi
Keaton
Keenan
Kehlani

Keiana
Keiko
Kelby
Kendyl
Kenia
Kentley
Kenzy
Keris
Keshet
Kesi
Khadijah
Khaleesi
Kharlia
Kiara
Kielo
Kimora
Kindra

Kinslee
Kiranda
Kitlyn
Korra
Krichelle
Kriska
Krizia
Krysia
Ksana
Kviiilyn
Kwyn
Kyndall
Kyniska
Kyomi
Kyrielle
Kyrilla
Kyuara

L

Labrenna
Lachesis
Lada
Laiz
Lakisha
Lapeka
Lapis
Latitia
Latrice
Layan
Leelee
Leelo
Leianna
Leire

Leoline
Leondrea
Liadan
Lieke
Liesl
Lilavati
Liliosa
Lilo
Lindezza
Liviana
Livy
Lizeth
Lorin
Lottchen

Lotye
Lovelyn
Loxley
Luanda
Lubov
Lucasta
Lucija
Luella
Lumi
Lumina
Luvenia

Luxi
Lyja
Lykke
Lynley
Lynnee
Lynwen
Lyra
Lysandra
Lystra
Lyyt

M

Maat
Maaza
Macon
Madigan
Madrigal
Maelle
Maelys
Maeryn
Maeve
Magaidh
Magnilde
Maile
Makeda
Malani
Maliyah
Mamie
Mandisa
Mareike
Margolo
Marley

Marlowe
Meditrina
Mehira
Meilani
Melika
Melisande
Mellie
Mererid
Meriel
Micaiah
Mika
Mila
Miloslava
Miri
Mistelle
Mitra
Moa
Morgause
Morise
Morrisania

Morwenna
Musetta
Muta
Mycella
Myeshia

Myfanwy
Mylah
Myrilla
Myrrhine

N

Nadege
Nadenka
Nadeyn
Nadezda
Nahla
Naia
Naiara
Najah
Najila
Nakotah
Nalani
Nariah
Nashira
Nathaly
Nava
Navaeh
Nayeli
Naylani
Nazanin
Nechama
Neda
Neela
Nefertiti
Nekane
Nelda

Nerissa
Nerys
Nettie
Nevena
Nevy
Ngaio
Nika
Nikeesha
Nilani
Niobe
Niyah
Niylah
Nizana
Noe
Noelani
Nour
Novalyne
Nuala
Nuray
Nuri
Nya
Nyala
Nyree
Nzingha

O

Oakley
Oana
Ocie
Odalis
Oddveig
Odeda
Odelene
Odila
Ohana
Okalani
Oksana
Olesia
Oliana
Olivienne
Olivine
Olwyn
Olyssa
Omarosa
Ombra
Onari
Ondine
Oneonta
Onika
Onyx
Ophira

Oralee
Oria
Oriana
Oriane
Orla
Orlagh
Orlena
Orli
Ormanda
Orna
Orsola
Osanna
Osha
Oska
Osla
Ottavia
Ottilia
Ouida
Ouisa
Ovidia
Owena
Ozara
Ozette
Ozma

P

Pacifica
Paisley
Pakwa
Pallas

Paloma
Pamina
Panteha
Panya

Paphos
Paquita
Parca
Parisa
Pascala
Patience
Pax
Paz
Paza
Pazice
Pearl
Peigi
Pema
Penelope
Peony
Persis
Perzsike
Petal
Petra
Petrina
Petronella

Petronia
Philida
Philomena
Phoenix
Pia
Pietra
Pilar
Piper
Pippa
Poet
Polina
Pomona
Poppy
Precious
Primrose
Princess
Prisca
Prospera
Puebla
Pyrene

Q

Qasey
Qigi
Qisya
Qmara
Quandra
Quartney
Queen
Queena
Queenie
Queleigh

Quelina
Quelle
Quenby
Quenna
Quentessa
Querida
Querube
Queta
Quetsalesk
Quetsali

Quetzaly
Quiana
Quieva
Quilian
Quilla
Quimoy
Quinby
Quincee
Quincy
Quindelia
Quineta
Quinlan
Quinn
Quinna
Quinnie

Quinnley
Quinta
Quintessa
Quintina
Quinzel
Quirien
Quisha
Quiterie
Quninleigh
Quorra
Quynh
Quynn
Qwynn
Qynnh

R

Rabanne
Rabiah
Radhiya
Raee
Raegan
Rafa
Raffaclla
Rahab
Raina
Raisa
Ramira
Randa
Reese
Reginy
Reiko
Reinette

Remi
Ren
Renata
Reseda
Reshma
Reta
Rcvcl
Reverie
Reyna
Rez
Rhea
Rheya
Rica
Ridley
Rigby
Rina

Rio

River

Riya

Rocco

Rocio

Roderica

Romilly

Rosabel

Rowan

Rowena

Roxie

Rubi

Ruhee

Rylea

Ryleigh

Rylie

Ryo

S

Saam

Saanvi

Saba

Sabine

Sable

Sabra

Sabrielle

Saffi

Saffron

Saige

Sakari

Saniya

Sansa

Sasha

Saylor

Schuyler

Scotlynn

Selah

Selby

Seneca

Septima

Sera

Serafina

Serhilda

Shaelan

Shahla

Shaniece

Shasta

Shenandoah

Sheridan

Sidra

Siena

Sima

Sinead

Siobhan

Skyla

Skyler

Skylnne

Sloane

Socorro

Star

Stockard

Suki

Suma

Sunniva
Suri
Suvi

Svetlana
Sydnee

T

Tabassum
Tabata
Tabatha
Tabby
Tabia
Tabrett
Taina
Taja
Taleen
Taliah
Talitha
Tamia
Tana
Tanisha
Tansy
Taryne
Tawney
Taya
Tebetha
Teegan
Tempest
Tenaya
Tenley
Tennie
Texanna

Thea
Theofania
Theresia
Thessaly
Tiara
Tiarna
Tinley
Tinsley
Tirzah
Tiziana
Tova
Towanda
Tressa
Trinity
Truelian
Trysta
Tully
Twila
Tyala
Tyla
Tyra
Tyreena
Tzeitel
Tzuria

U

Udelia
Udile
Uhura
Ujvala
Ulalume
Ulani
Uleema
Uli
Ulka
Ulrika
Ululani
Ulvhild
Ulyana
Uma
Umaira
Umaiza
Umali
Umay
Umayal
Umber
Umbrielle
Umme
Ummu
Umniah
Unathi

Undine
Unice
Unita
Unity
Unni
Urassaya
Urbana
Urbi
Urelia
Uri
Uriela
Ursina
Ursule
Ursulina
Urszula
Urte
Urvi
Usha
Ustinya
Uswa
Uta
Uulrica
Uxue
Uzma

V

Vada
Vadamae
Vaetild
Vaila

Valda
Valdis
Valen
Valentina

Valeska
Vali
Vallea
Vanda
Vanora
Vanya
Varsha
Varya
Vasiliki
Veda
Vedette
Veerie
Velvet
Venetia
Verbenia
Verdi
Verena
Verity
Verochka
Veronique
Vianne

Vicenza
Vida
Vienna
Viera
Vijaya
Viktorie
Vimala
Virag
Virdia
Viridiana
Viridienne
Viveca
Vivi
Vivia
Vivica
Vlada
Vladka
Vladlena
Vor
Vrai

W

Wadeema
Wai
Wallis
Walynn
Wanaka
Waneta
Wanipa
Wanjiru
Wardah
Waverly

Wejdan
Welles
Wendla
Wendolyn
Wesleigh
Westlynne
Weylyn
Whimsy
Wietske
Wilaysia

Wilde
Willa
Willabelle
Willodean
Willoh
Wilmary
Wilsonia
Winley
Winnie
Winola
Winonah
Winslet
Winsley

Winslow
Wisteria
Witt
Wraelyn
Wrenley
Wrenna
Wrynley
Wylda
Wylee
Wylla
Wynita
Wynn
Wyomia

X

Xabelle
Xabrina
Xael
Xaiya
Xallma
Xander
Xandra
Xantara
Xanthe
Xanthea
Xanthippe
Xanthis
Xavia
Xavianna
Xavierre
Xen
Xena

Xenia
Xenobia
Xhivani
Xhosa
Xia
Xiamara
Xiker
Ximena
Xin
Xiola
Xiomara
Xiomya
Xion
Xionara
Xiou
Xitali
Xochie

Xoey
Xois
Xosha
Xuen
Xuriya
Xuxa
Xylah
Xylda

Xyleena
Xyliana
Xylona
Xymeria
Xyra
Xyzah
Xzonia

Y

Vysabel
Yadira
Yaeko
Yaffa
Yahaira
Yajaita
Yamila
Yamini
Yana
Yanamarie
Yaneli
Yara
Yanet
Yani
Yareli
Yasmeen
Yaya
Yazmyne
Yekaterina
Yelena
Yemina
Yessenia
Yevdokiya

Yocheved
Yoneko
Yoobin
Yoselin
Yoshie
Youna
Ysabeau
Ysabella
Ysela
Ysobele
Yue
Yuki
Yukia
Yulia
Yuliana
Yulissa
Yumi
Yunoka
Yurika
Yustina
Yuzu
Yvaine
Yvanna

Yvie

Yvonna

Yvoni

Z

Zafira

Zabana

Zada

Zadie

Zahara

Zahra

Zahraa

Zaida

Zaina

Zainab

Zaira

Zaire

Zakia

Zandra

Zanne

Zara

Zarah

Zariah

Zarina

Zariyah

Zaya

Zayda

Zaylee

Zaynab

Zeina

Zella

Zelma

Zen

Zenaida

Zendaya

Zenovia

Zephyr

Zhane

Zhavia

Zhuri

Zia

Ziggy

Zilpah

Zion

Zipporah

Zirae

Ziva

Ziya

Zoie

Zola

Zora

Zoya

Zuri

Zyla

FEMALE NICKNAMES

Amazon
Angel
Babe
Babycakes
Babydoll
Bambi
Barbie
Beanie
Bebe
Berry
Birdie
Bitsy
Blondie
Blossom
Blueberry
Bonbon
Bubbles
Bug
Bunny
Buttercup
Butterfly
Button
Candy
Cherry Blossom
Chica
Chickadee
Chipmunk
Cinderella
Cinnamon

Coco
Cookie
Cosmo
Cowgirl
Cricket
Cuddles
Cupcake
Cupid
Cutie Pie
Daisy
Darling
Dearest
Dearie
Dewdrop
Dimples
Diva
Doll
Dove
Dragonfly
Duchess
Ducky
Dumpling
Firecracker
Firefly
Foxy
Freckles
Gem
Genie
Goddess

Goldie
Goldilocks
Grasshopper
Gumdrop
Half Pint
Heaven
Holly
Honey
Honeybee
Honeybun
Honeypot
Honeysuckle
Hot Cakes
Hot Stuff
Huckleberry
Hun
Jelly
Jellybean
Jewel
Jujube
Kitten
Kitty
Lady Bug
Lamb Chop
Lilly
Lollipop
Love
Lucky Charm
Marshmallow
Milady
Mimi
Minion
Missy
Monkey

Moonbeam
Moonshine
Mouse
Muffin
Nugget
Nutty
Panda
Peaches
Peanut
Pebbles
Pickle
Pineapple
Pinky
Polly
Posy
Princess
Prissy
Pumpkin
Punkin
Queen
Raindrop
Rebel
Red
Rockstar
Rosie
Shadow
Shortcake
Sky
Snookie
Sparkles
Spicy
Spirit
Squishy
Star

Starlight
Sugar
Summer
Sunflower
Sunny
Sunshine
Sweet cheeks
Sweetheart
Sweet pea
Sweets
Sweetums
Teddy

Tiger
Tigress
Tinkerbell
Tootsie
Treasure
Tulip
Tweetie
Tweetums
Twinkie
Unicorn
Venus

UNUSUAL MALE NAMES

A

Aarav
Abbot
Abdel
Abel
Abelard
Abram
Ackley
Acton
Adair
Addis
Adel
Adnan
Adrian
Adriel
Aesir
Aeson
Ahearn
Aiden
Aiken
Ajax
Akiba
Alano
Albin
Aldric
Alfarin

Ambrose
Amir
Andrik
Ansel
Apollo
Aram
Archer
Ardell
Ari
Arik
Ario
Arro
Ascot
Asher
Ashton
Audwin
August
Avi
Awan
Axel
Ayaan
Ayers
Aylwin
Azriel

B

Babel

Bader

Bakari

Bambino

Bao

Baris

Barrett

Barron

Basha

Batu

Baylor

Beauden

Beckett

Benaiah

Benicio

Bennett

Bentlee

Benton

Bishop

Boaz

Bodhi

Bodie

Bohdi

Booker

Boone

Bora

Bowie

Brantley

Braxton

Braxtyn

Braylen

Brecken

Brentley

Brice

Bridger

Briggs

Briscoe

Bristol

Britton

Brix

Brixton

Brock

Brogan

Bronson

Bryar

Bryden

Brysen

Bryton

Bryze

C

Cace

Cadell

Cadwik

Caelan

Caine

Calder

Camilo

Carden

Carnell
Cashel
Cassian
Cayson
Caz
Chanan
Chaz
Cheney
Chiko
Cian
Cillian
Cisco
Clarion
Cleavon
Clovis
Cochise
Coen
Cohen
Coleman
Collier
Colm

Conall
Conary
Connla
Conran
Conyn
Corban
Cortez
Craven
Cray
Creighton
Crespin
Crew
Crichton
Cristobal
Cuinn
Curro
Cy
Cyrano
Cyrax
Cyrek

D

Daan
Dacian
Dacken
Daegan
Daelan
Dak
Damari
Dangelo
Danton
Daoud

Dario
Darroch
Davi
Davon
Davu
Daxton
Daylin
Dayson
Dedrick
Deegan

Degory
Deniz
Deon
Deron
Deshan
Dev
Devan
Deverell
Deylin
Dimka
Dionysys
Dix
Dolphus
Donal
Donato

Donte
Dorset
Draxler
Drexel
Drystan
Duald
Duccio
Dundee
Dunmore
Dunstan
Durward
Dwade
Dweezil
Dyson

E

Ean
Earnes
Eastman
Easton
Ebb
Edsel
Edvin
Eiger
Elad
Eldra
Elian
Elijas
Elisea
Eliseo
Elling
Elmore

Elric
Elyas
Emeka
Emerson
Emiel
Emil
Emmitt
Emory
Emric
Emrys
Eno
Enoch
Ensley
Enzo
Ephraim
Erhard

Erich
Erst
Erwin
Esaias
Espen
Essa
Esteban
Esten
Ethen

Evander
Everette
Everly
Evron
Ezio
Ezra
Ezrah
Ezri

F

Faaris
Fabi
Fabian
Fabrizio
Fadi
Fadil
Falan
Faraz
Fareed
Farhan
Farid
Faris
Farley
Farryll
Farzam
Farzan
Fausto
Favian
Fedor
Felyx
Feng
Fenton

Fenwick
Fergie
Fergus
Ferguson
Ferrier
Ferrill
Festus
Filmore
Fineas
Finlay
Finlea
Finnbar
Finncas
Finnian
Finnick
Fintan
Flint
Flynn
Fonzie
Forrest
Frans
Fraser

Fulton
Fyffe
Fynley

Fynn
Fynnigan

G

Gaddiel
Gaeton
Gaige
Gaius
Gamaliel
Garner
Garrick
Garwood
Gavin
Gavino
Gawaine
Gawen
Gennadi
Geno
Gentry
Gergor
Gerrit
Giancarlo
Gianni
Gib
Gibson
Gil
Gimle
Gino
Gio

Girvyn
Giuliano
Gladwin
Glyn
Godric
Godwyn
Gorman
Gowyn
Gradon
Grady
Granvill
Graysen
Greely
Grenville
Griffin
Griffith
Grover
Gru
Gunder
Gunnar
Gunther
Gustaof
Gwern
Gwilym

H

Hadar
Hadden
Hadley
Hadrien
Hael
Hafgrim
Hagley
Haiden
Haim
Haines
Haji
Hal
Halden
Halford
Hamish
Hannibal
Hanno
Harbin
Harden
Harding
Haris
Harme
Hayden
Heaton
Heike

Helix
Helmut
Hendrix
Henley
Herne
Hieronymus
Hilal
Hillel
Hobart
Holden
Hollis
Holman
Holmes
Hrut
Hu
Hubertus
Huck
Hudson
Humbert
Hume
Hyde
Hyder
Hyman
Hyperion

I

Ibrahim
Icarus
Ido
Idris

Iggie
Ignace
Ignacio
Ignati

Ignatius

Ikaros

Ilya

Iman

Imani

Imray

Inam

Inar

Indy

Ingamar

Ingo

Ingram

Irfan

Irvin

Isaac

Isacco

Isael

Isai

Isandro

Ishaan

Isham

Ishan

Ishmael

Isidoro

Isidro

Iskender

Issa

Itamar

Itzhak

Ivanhoe

Ivano

Ivarr

Iver

Ivica

Ivo

Iwan

Iyyar

Izak

Izayah

Izmael

Izz

J

Jabari

Jabin

Jacek

Jachin

Jacobo

Jagger

Jahan

Jakobe

Jameel

Jango

Jaren

Jarick

Jarrell

Jarvis

Jaskaran

Jatan

Jaxton

Jaxx

Jaydan

Jaydin

Jaylon
Jayven
Jeddiah
Jenner
Jeppe
Jess
Joachin
Jodin
Jonn
Jordi
Jori
Josef
Joshuah
Josiah
Joss

Jovi
Joziah
Jozy
Judah
Judd
Judson
Julen
Junius
Jurj
Jussi
Justice
Juwan
Jye
Jyn

K

Kaapo
Kabir
Kadar
Kael
Kaelan
Kagam
Kai
Kairo
Kaiser
Kalan
Kam
Kamil
Kanren
Keaghan
Keanan
Keanu

Keene
Keiran
Kek
Kelby
Kelyn
Kemen
Kennan
Kenton
Kenzie
Keon
Keyon
Khalil
Khan
Kian
Kiefer
Kiernan

Kildare
Kingsley
Klas
Knox
Knut
Kobe
Kohen
Koi
Konstantin

Korbin
Korian
Kort
Kyan
Kye
Kylan
Kyler
Kynon

L

Laban
Ladomir
Lael
Laird
Lancaster
Lancel
Landon
Landyn
Laramie
Lark
Lathan
Lazaro
Lazarus
Leandro
Ledger
Legend
Leib
Leif
Leighton
Leland
Lem
Lenox
Leonato

Leonel
Leopold
Levi
Linc
Liron
Lito
Llewyn
Llyr
Loch
Lochlan
Lochran
Lowell
Lowen
Loyal
Luc
Lucan
Lucca
Lucien
Ludovic
Lugh
Lyle
Lyman
Lyndon

Lynx
Lyon

Lyric

M

Maachi
Maddox
Madhav
Magnus
Maison
Makari
Maksim
Malakai
Malek
Marcelo
Marek
Mariano
Marino
Marlon
Marquis
Marwan
Maur
Mauricio
Maxime
Maximiliamo
Maxton
Maxx
Mayson
McKinley
Medwyn

Meino
Melbyrne
Melvin
Mendel
Mercer
Merrick
Mica
Mikah
Mikhail
Miko
Milo
Minh
Misael
Mischa
Mitchell
Montez
Morse
Muhd
Muni
Munroe
Murdock
Mustafa
Mylo
Myrick

N

Nadeem
Nader

Naji
Nakoa

Nanak
Narmir
Nasr
Natanael
Naveen
Navid
Navon
Nazareth
Nazir
Nehemiah
Neiko
Neilan
Nemo
Nestor
Nev
Nevaeh
Nevins
Newel
Neper
Newlin
Neymar
Niels
Nihit

Nikan
Nikander
Niki
Nikos
Nil
Nile
Nilo
Nils
Nixon
Nirvan
Nivin
Nizar
Noam
Noble
Noe
Noll
Noor
Norberto
Nori
Norwin
Novah
Nuno

O

Oak
Oakley
Oan
Obed
Oberon
Obert
Obi
Obie

Ocia
Octa
Ode
Odhran
Odilon
Odin
Odissan
Odonata

Ogden

Ohan

Ojai

Olavi

Oleg

Olin

Oliverio

Olof

Olufemi

Omer

Omid

Oneal

Oran

Ordell

Orev

Orlin

Orrel

Orsino

Orton

Orval

Oshea

Osheen

Osher

Oskar

Osmar

Ossin

Oswin

Othmar

Othniel

Otto

Ovie

Oziel

Ozzie

P

Paavo

Pacio

Packer

Padgett

Palmer

Parrie

Parris

Pascoe

Pasquale

Paulo

Payce

Pazel

Pedayel

Pedram

Pedrio

Peeta

Pekka

Peleg

Pell

Penley

Perdido

Peregrine

Pernell

Petr

Petre

Petrus

Pharrell

Philo

Phineas
Phons
Pickford
Pierino
Piero
Pierre
Piet
Pilsen
Platt
Pollux
Pontus

Pramesh
Pramod
Pratt
Prem
Prentiss
Prestley
Princeton
Procopio
Pryce
Pwyll

Q

Qadar
Qadeer
Qadim
Qaim
Qais
Qaizer
Qayden
Qhama
Qhawe
Qi
Qintain
Quade
Quang
Quang
Quiston
Quantez
Quantrell
Quarry
Quasai
Quatrain

Quaveon
Quavious
Quay
Que
Quel
Quennel
Quest
Quigley
Quillan
Quilo
Quimby
Quince
Quindlen
Quinlan
Quinnell
Quinson
Quint
Quinton
Quintrell
Quintus

Quirin

Quirino

Quirinus

Quirt

Quixley

Qunten

Quon

Qusay

Qyennel

R

Ra

Rabi

Racer

Radley

Rafi

Raidon

Raj

Rakin

Raleigh

Rally

Rankin

Rawson

Rayan

Rei

Remus

Remy

Renzo

Rey

Reza

Rhesus

Rhys

Rico

Ridgely

Ridley

Riel

Riggan

River

Roan

Roano

Roc

Rockley

Roderick

Rodion

Roka

Rolfe

Rolo

Ronan

Ronell

Ronin

Rorik

Ross

Roth

Rousse

Ruadhagan

Ruddy

Rudyard

Rufus

Ryden

Rye

S

Sabien
Sadler
Safa
Sagan
Sakari
Salvatore
Samir
Sanders
Sandro
Santos
Sawyer
Saxon
Schroeder
Schylar
Scooter
Scorpio
Seager
Secric
Sexton
Shai
Shamus
Shaw
Shedrick
Shepard
Shia

Shiva
Shola
Shon
Shukri
Shye
Sigvard
Sitka
Skylar
Slater
Slayde
Sorin
Spyridon
Stearns
Stiles
Stockholm
Stoney
Strider
Swinton
Sy
Syed
Sykes
Sylas
Szcrepan
Szymon

T

Taavetti
Tabbart
Tadashi
Tadeo

Tag
Tai
Taj
Takoda

Talbot
Tamar
Tariq
Taro
Tavon
Taylon
Tedric
Telek
Telford
Tennyson
Thane
Theodrik
Theron
Thorald
Thurstan
Tibault
Tibor
Tierney
Titus
Tobyn
Todrick

Tolan
Tomek
Topi
Tor
Toren
Torsten
Traugott
Treven
Tristam
Trygve
Trystan
Tusya
Twiford
Tyce
Tydeus
Tyr
Tyree
Tyrell
Tyrus
Tzadok

U

Ubaydah
Uchechi
Udai
Udell
Udi
Udith
Udo
Udoka
Udolf
Ugo

Ugochukwu
Ujaan
Ukiah
Ulan
Ulisses
Ulric
Ultan
Umar
Umaryr
Umber

Umer
Unika
Unni
Unwinn
Updyke
Upshaw
Upton
Upwood
Urban
Uriah
Uriel
Urien
Urki
Urso
Ursus

Urvil
Usher
Ushi
Usku
Usman
Usuherdene
Uther
Uthman
Uttam
Uyanga
Uz
Uzayr
Uziah
Uzziah

V

Vaden
Vadhir
Vale
Valentin
Vallen
Valor
Vander
Vann
Vansh
Varad
Varden
Varro
Varun
Vaughn
Vava
Vedanth

Vedran
Vel
Verge
Vermont
Vernell
Vernen
Vetri
Vidal
Vidur
Viggo
Vihaan
Vijay
Vikram
Vinayak
Vincenzo
Vinh

Vini
Vinson
Vinzent
Viraj
Viransh
Virgil
Vishnu
Vishyalii
Vita

Vito
Vitus
Vivek
Vrishank
Vu
Vuk
Vyan
Vyom

W

Wain
Wainwright
Waite
Waldron
Walford
Walfred
Walid
Warrick
Wasim
Watt
Waverlee
Way
Webb
Welden
Wenceslaus
Wenzel
Westleigh
Wharton
Whitelaw
Wick
Wil
Wilbert

Wilf
Wilfredo
Willem
Willkie
Wilmar
Wilmer
Wim
Win
Windom
Wingate
Winslow
Winston
Winton
Witold
Wladyslaw
Wolcott
Wolfram
Woodrow
Worden
Wulfric
Wyclef
Wyeth

Wylei
Wyler
Wynton

Wyre
Wystan

X

Xade
Xadianni
Xae
Xaelyn
Xai
Xaida
Xailee
Xaire
Xamori
Xander
Xandrei
Xandria
Xandros
Xanthus
Xavi
Xavian
Xaviell
Xaviero
Xavion
Xaylen
Xayne
Xena
Xeno
Xenon
Xenophon

Xenos
Xerxes
Xever
Xi
Xiao
Xiaoxiao
Xidom
Ximenez
Xin
Xiomara
Xion
Xixi
Xolani
Xristodoulos
Xu
Xuan
Xun
Xuri
Xy
Xyion
Xyon
Xyz
Xzavier
Xzayden

Y

Yaakov

Yacoub

Yadiel

Yahir

Yahti

Yahya

Yair

Yakim

Yancy

Yannis

Yantz

Yaron

Yasha

Yasha

Yasiel

Yavin

Yavor

Ybarra

Yehuda

Yehudi

Yered

Yevgeny

Yeziel

Yienio

Yisroel

Yissachar

Yoanis

Yoel

Yonah

Yonatan

Yordani

Yorick

Yoruba

Youking

Ysidro

Yubal

Yukio

Yul

Yulieskis

Yuma

Yuniers

Yura

Yurek

Yuri

Yurik

Yusef

Yuuto

Yves

Ywain

Z

Zade

Zadock

Zaen

Zafar

Zaid

Zaire

Zakariya

Zaki

Zakk

Zale

Zalman

Zameer

Zan

Zayd

Zayle

Zebulun

Zedrick

Zeff

Zekariah

Zeke

Zelig

Zenon

Zenos

Zephan

Zer

Zeref

Zev

Zevon

Zinovi

Ziv

Zivon

Ziyad

Zlatan

Zoilo

Zon

Zoran

Zoravar

Zotique

Zsolt

Zuberi

Zuhair

Zuko

Zuma

Zuriel

Zvonko

Zylen

Zyler

Zyon

Zzyzx

MALE NICKNAMES

Ace
Alpha
Amigo
Angus
Babe
Babysaurus
Bad Kitty
Bae
Batman
Bear
Beast
Beau
Bellissimo
Big Guy
Big Mac
Boo
Boss
Boy Toy
Brainiac
Braveheart
Buckeye
Buddy
Bumpkin
Cadillac
Captain
Carebear
Casanova

Champ
Charming
Chewbaca
Chief
Colossus
Cowboy
Daddy Mack
Daredevil
Daring
Darling
Dear
Don Juan
Duck
Fabio
Fella
Firecracker
Flame
Fox
Gladiator
Godzilla
Goof
Goofball
Gordo
Granite
Hammer
Hawk
Hercules

Hero

Hon

Honey

Honey Bear

Hot Stuff

Hotshot

Huggy Bear

Hulk

Hun Bun

Hunk

Iceman

Iron Man

Jelly Bear

Jigsaw

Jock

Jockey

Judge

Ket Kat

Kid

King

Knight

Lady Killer

Lefty

Lemon Drop

Love Machine

Love Muffin

Lover

Loverboy

Mad Jack

Marshmallow

Maverick

Meatball

Merlin

Mister

Muffin

Munchkin

Neo

Nibbles

Ninja

Nutty

Old Man

Omega

Panda Bear

Peanut

Pickles

Pitbull

Popeye

Prince

Psycho

Puma

Puppy

Quackers

Querido

Red

Rider

Righty

Robin Hood

Rockstar

Romeo

Sailor

Scooter

Shadow

Shorty

Slick

Snickerdoodle

Snuggy

Spanky

Sparky

Sport

Strider

Stud

Superman

Superstar

T-Rex

Taco

Tarzan

Teddy Bear

Thunder Cat

Tiger

Tiny

Treasure

Untamed

Vegas

Viking

Warrior

WinkyDink

Wolverine

Wonka

Woody

Wookie

Yankee

Zeus

Zorro

LAST NAMES

A

Abbey
Abbott
Abercrombie
Abernathy
Ables
Abner
Abrams
Ackerman
Ackroyd
Adair
Adamson
Adcock
Adleman
Adler
Adrian
Agnew
Aguilar
Ahearn
Alanso
Albert
Albright
Alder
Aldrich
Alexander
Allen

Allred
Alston
Altman
Alvarez
Anderson
Andrews
Aniston
Ansay
Ansley
Anson
Applebaum
Appling
Archer
Armstrong
Arndt
Arnold
Arvin
Ash
Atkinson
Atwood
Augustine
Avery
Avi
Ayres

B

Babbitt

Bach

Bagley

Baker

Baldwin

Balkman

Ballard

Banks

Bannister

Barbosa

Barker

Barkley

Barnes

Beck

Bedford

Bellamy

Bender

Bennett

Benson

Bergen

Bigelow

Billingsley

Bing

Birch

Bishop

Blackwell

Blake

Blanco

Bolden

Bond

Booker

Boone

Bowie

Boyd

Brackins

Bradley

Bragg

Braun

Brewer

Brooks

Bryant

Buckner

Bullard

Burgos

Burke

Burns

Burton

Butler

Byrnes

C

Caballero

Cable

Caffey

Cage

Calabrese

Caldwell

Calloway

Cambridge

Campbell
Castillo
Castro
Chamberlain
Chan
Chandler
Chaney
Chang
Chavez
Chen
Cheng
Chiang
Childress
Ching
Clavell
Cofield
Coker
Coleman
Collier
Collins
Collinsworth

Colson
Colter
Conley
Contreras
Cortez
Costello
Covington
Cox
Craig
Crawford
Crispin
Crocker
Croft
Crow
Crutchfield
Cruz
Cummings
Cunningham
Curran
Curry

D

Dailey
Dallmar
Daniels
Darcey
Darnell
Darrow
Daugherty
Daves
Davidson
Davis

Dawson
De la Cruz
De Leon
Delaney
Delfino
Delgado
Dempsey
Denning
Denton
Devlin

Diaz
Dickens
Dickerson
Dillard
Dillon
Dinnel
Dixon
Dodd
Dominguez
Donaldson
Dong
Donovan
Dorsey
Dotson

Douglas
Dover
Downey
Doyle
Dozier
Drexler
Driscoll
Dudley
Duffy
Dumas
Dunham
Durant
Dyson
Drew

E

Eads
Eady
Eagan
Earl
Easley
Eastman
Easton
Ebert
Ebner
Ecker
Eddie
Edgerson
Edison
Edmondson
Edwards
Edwin
Egerson

Egger
Elder
Eldred
Eldridge
Elert
Ellery
Ellington
Elliott
Ellis
Ellsworth
Elmer
Elsinger
Elwin
Emerson
Emery
Emmett
Engel

English
Engstrom
Erickson
Escamilla
Esparza
Espinoza
Essert
Estes

Esteves
Estrada
Evans
Everett
Everhart
Everly
Ezra

F

Farmer
Farrell
Faulkner
Felix
Fellows
Fells
Felton
Feng
Ferguson
Fernandez
Ferry
Fields
Fife
Fillmore
Finley
Fischer
Fitch
Fitzgerald
Fitzpatrick
Fizer
Flemings
Fletcher
Flint

Flores
Flowers
Floyd
Flynn
Fong
Fontaine
Ford
Foreman
Forrest
Forte
Forth
Fortson
Foster
Fowler
Fox
Foyle
Francis
Franklin
Fray
Frazer
Fredrick
Freeman
Frye

Fuentes
Fuji

Fuller

G

Gadsen
Gaffney
Gaines
Gamble
Garcia
Gardner
Garnett
Garrett
Garrison
Garza
Gatling
Gayden
Geary
Genji
George
Gibson
Gil
Gilchrist
Gilder
Giles
Givens
Glover
Golden
Goldwin
Goldwire

Gomez
Gonzales
Gooden
Goodrich
Goodwin
Gordon
Grace
Graham
Granger
Graves
Greene
Greenway
Greer
Gregory
Grey
Grier
Griffin
Griffith
Grimes
Grimm
Grundy
Guerrero
Gutierrez
Guzman

H

Haku
Hamilton

Hammonds
Hancock

Hansen
Hardin
Hardt
Hardy
Harper
Harrington
Harris
Harrison
Harvey
Hashioto
Hassell
Hawkins
Haywood
Heath
Henderson
Hendrix
Hernandez
Herrera
Hess
Hibbert
Hicks
Hidalgo
Hill

Hines
Hodges
Holcombe
Holiday
Holland
Hollis
Holmes
Hood
Horner
Horsely
Horton
Houston
Howard
Hsiung
Huang
Hudson
Huff
Huffman
Hughes
Humphries
Hunter
Hurley

I

Ianni
Iati
Ibarra
Ibert
Ibok
Ibrahim
Idell
Idenhen

Idlet
Idol
Idris
Iglesias
Ike
Ikuno
Iles
Imes

Imhoff

Imholt

Imperati

Impero

Ines

Inge

Ingelsby

Ingersoll

Ingerson

Ingle

Ingles

Ingraham

Ingram

Ipsley

Irby

Ireland

Ireton

Irons

Ironside

Irvin

Irvine

Irving

Irwin

Isaacks

Isakson

Isbell

Isler

Isley

Issard

Iverson

Ivey

Ivory

Izzo

J

Jackman

Jackson

Jacobs

Jacobson

Jacques

Jaeger

Jagger

James

Jamison

Janeway

Jans

Jarrett

Jarvis

Jasper

Jeffers

Jefferson

Jeffries

Jekell

Jenifer

Jenkins

Jenks

Jenner

Jennings

Jernigan

Jerome

Jerrells

Jesse

Jessen

Jeter
Jewell
Jimenez
Jobs
Johansen
Johnson
Joiner
Jolly
Jones
Jonus
Jordan

Joseph
Joslin
Joyce
Joyner
Juarez
Judd
Judge
Jukes
Julian
Juxson

K

Kamp
Kane
Kanne
Karl
Karn
Kartchner
Kato
Kawasaki
Keating
Keefe
Keene
Keith
Keller
Kelley
Kellogg
Kendrick
Kennedy
Kent
Kerr
Kerry

Kessler
Keys
Kidd
Kiefer
Kilgore
Killingsworth
Kim
Kimble
Kimura
Kincade
King
Kingsbury
Kinnard
Kirk
Kirkland
Kirkpatrick
Klein
Knight
Knipp
Knowles

Knox
Koch
Kody
Kohn
Kramer

Krause
Kuhn
Kurtz
Kyles

L

Lacey
Laird
Landry
Lane
Langdon
Langford
Langley
Lao
Lattimore
Lauren
Laurie
Lavender
Law
Lawrence
Lawson
Leach
Leary
Lee
Leon
Leonard
Lewis
Li
Liang
Lim
Lindner

Lindsay
Little
Liu
Livingston
Lloyd
Locke
Lockett
Lodge
Loewe
Lofton
Logan
London
Long
Lopez
Lorenzo
Love
Lovett
Lowry
Lucas
Ludwig
Luna
Lutz
Lynch
Lyons

M

Mack
Mackenzie
Macon
Maddox
Madsen
Major
Malone
Mann
Marin
Marquez
Marshall
Martin
Martinez
Mason
Matsumoto
Matthews
Maxwell
May
Mayberry
McCoy
McFarland
McGee
McGuire
McNeal
Medina

Meeks
Mendez
Mendoza
Mercer
Miles
Miller
Mills
Millsap
Mitchell
Mobley
Molina
Moore
Morales
Moreno
Morris
Morrison
Morrow
Morton
Mullin
Munoz
Murdock
Murphy
Murray
Myers

N

Nabors
Nagle
Nakamura
Nance

Napier
Napp
Nash
Nathan

Navarro
Neale
Neaton
Needham
Neison
Nelham
Nelson
Neptune
Nesbitt
Nesby
Neve
Nevill
Neward
Newbury
Newman
Newton
Ng
Nicholas
Nicholson
Nightingale
Nix

Nixon
Noah
Noble
Noell
Nolte
Noonan
Noriega
Norman
Norridge
Norris
North
Northgate
Norwood
Nottingham
Novak
Nume
Nunez
Nutt
Nutter
Nutton

O

Oades
Oakes
Oakley
Oates
Oatman
Ochs
Ockerman
Odell
Oden
Odom

Odum
Odway
Ogden
Oglesby
Okator
Okey
Okorie
Okosa
Oldham
Oldsworth

Oleary
Olinger
Oliver
Oliverson
Ollie
Olsen
Ommen
Oneal
Oppland
Orr
Ortega
Ortiz
Orton
Orvis
Orwell

Osbourne
Osby
Osgood
Osland
Ost
Ostler
Otis
Ott
Ottrix
Outlaw
Overbridge
Overton
Owens
Owsley

P

Packer
Packton
Paddock
Padgett
Paine
Painter
Pallson
Palmer
Parbridge
Parish
Parker
Peale
Pearson
Peckinham
Peco
Pedersen

Peele
Peerman
Pegg
Peirce
Pellham
Pena
Pennyman
Perez
Pheasant
Phellps
Phillips
Pickering
Pigg
Pillard
Pinck
Pine

Pinnick

Pittman

Playford

Poole

Poppin

Portman

Powell

Powers

Pratt

Price

Prickett

Prince

Proctor

Proudlove

Puckle

Pufford

Pye

Q

Qello

Quaid

Quake

Qualls

Quantock

Quaranta

Quarles

Quarrington

Quarry

Quartermaine

Quarterman

Quartlebaum

Quattro

Quattrocchi

Quayle

Quaynor

Queary

Queen

Queenan

Quejada

Quelch

Quenburow

Quenele

Quesenberry

Quezada

Quick

Quicksell

Quiette

Quigg

Quiggle

Quigley

Quill

Quilling

Quimby

Quinborow

Quincy

Quinlan

Quinn

Quinnett

Quinney

Quinones

Quint

Quintana

Quinto

Quinton

Quirke

Quisenberry
Quist

Qvale

R

Rabbitt
Raby
Radford
Ragdale
Ragge
Rainsford
Ramirez
Ramos
Ramridge
Ramsey
Rand
Randall
Ransom
Rashwell
Ratliff
Raymond
Reade
Redbird
Redding
Redgrave
Redshaw
Reed
Reeves
Rencocke
Reston

Retherford
Reycroft
Reyes
Rhodes
Rice
Richardson
Richman
Rickley
Ridge
Ripley
Rivera
Roberts
Robinson
Rodriguez
Roe
Rojas
Romero
Rosario
Rubio
Ruiz
Ruston
Ruthford
Ryland
Ryley

S

Saito

Salazar

Sampson
Sanchez
Sanders
Sanford
Santana
Santiago
Santos
Sanz
Sasaki
Sato
Scott
Serrano
Shackleford
Sharpe
Shaw
Sheppard
Shields
Shipman
Silva
Simmons
Simms
Simpkins
Singleton
Skinner

Slater
Slaughter
Smithe
Snow
Snyder
Sommerville
Soto
Spencer
Stackhouse
Staples
Stevenson
Stewart
Stockton
Stokes
Stone
Stout
Strickland
Suarez
Summers
Sutton
Suzuki
Sweetney
Swift

T

Talbott
Tallman
Tan
Tanaka
Tang
Tanner
Tasker

Tawney
Taylor
Tedbury
Tedman
Temple
Tennant
Tewbey

Thacker
Thatcher
Thomas
Thompson
Thornberry
Thorne
Thurgood
Tilly
Tippett
Toft
Tolley
Tollington
Tomkins
Tomlinson
Tonstall
Topping
Torres
Torte

Towers
Townley
Townsend
Travers
Treadwell
Treehill
Trible
Trindly
Tripp
Trotton
Trueblood
Trueman
Tryon
Tsou
Tucker
Tyler
Tyrrell

U

Ubel
Udall
Udi
Udoh
Udume
Uhi
Uhle
Ukah
Ukkleberg
Ulin
Ulman
Ulmer
Ulrich

Ultner
Ulysse
Umbel
Umberger
Umberhower
Umoren
Umpleby
Underhill
Underman
Underriner
Undersinger
Underwood
Union

Unseld
Upchurch
Updike
Uplinger
Upshaw
Upson
Urban
Urgo
Urias
Uribe
Urien
Ursery

Urso
Urwin
Usaker
Usera
Usher
Ussery
Uter
Uther
Uthoff
Utley
Utomi

V

Vaccaro
Vager
Vaile
Vainwrite
Valdez
Valentin
Valerio
Valliant
Vanbroke
Vance
Vandenburgh
Vandermash
Vane
Vanlove
Vargas
Varnon
Varsey
Vasquez
Vaughan

Veale
Vega
Velasco
Velasquez
Venables
Vennor
Ventura
Verity
Vernon
Verona
Ververs
Vickers
Victors
Vigo
Vincent
Viner
Viole
Violett
Vizard

Voigt
Volk
Voll
Vollet
Voronin
Voss

Vossen
Vowell
Voysden
Vybert
Vye

W

Wade
Wagner
Walker
Wallace
Walls
Walsh
Walton
Wang
Ward
Warrick
Washington
Watanabe
Watson
Weatherspoon
Weaver
Webber
Webster
Wei
Wells
Wesley
West
Westbrook
Whaley
Wheeler
Whisby

White
Whiteside
Whitworth
Wiens
Wilcox
Wilkins
Wilks
Williams
Willis
Willoughby
Wilmont
Wilson
Wingate
Wingfield
Winston
Winter
Witney
Wolfe
Wong
Woods
Woodside
Workman
Wright
Wu

X

Xaa
Xaereb
Xaio
Xalom
Xanders
Xanerich
Xanthopoulos
Xanthos
Xaramillo
Xash
Xaver
Xavier
Xayo
Xea
Xemmara
Xenakis
Xhari
Xi
Xia
Xianran
Xiao
Xiaolong
Xiciani
Xidias

Xigri
Ximenes
Ximines
Xing
Xinran
Xinsen
Xiong
Xiron
Xix
Xmas
Xolomiansky
Xrawczyk
Xstopher
Xu
Xua
Xuares
Xue
Xuliastres
Xun
Xutle
Xuz
Xxleavitt
Xygmti
Xylander

Y

Yackley
Yada
Yadrich
Yale
Yaleman

Yallopp
Yamada
Yamamoto
Yames
Yancey

Yanders
Yang
Yao
Yapp
Yarborough
Yarbury
Yard
Yardley
Yarne
Yarrow
Yarwell
Yates
Yazzie
Ybarra
Yeager
Yeamond
Yearby
Yearpin
Yearwood
Yeazel

Yeko
Yelder
Yelovich
Yeomans
Yeung
Yin
Yoe
Yoho
Yoneoto
Yong
York
Yoshda
Youmans
Young
Youngblood
Younger
Younker
Yowell
Yuan

Z

Zachery
Zack
Zager
Zahn
Zald
Zambrana
Zamora
Zamorano
Zampler
Zandbergen
Zaney

Zang
Zangari
Zaragoza
Zastrow
Zayas
Zazuri
Zeigler
Zeller
Zells
Zelly
Zeno

Zephyr

Zerbe

Zerkel

Zesterman

Zettle

Zhang

Zhao

Zick

Zidar

Zierden

Zimbro

Zimmerman

Zinny

Ziri

Zitani

Zito

Ziv

Zoellner

Zoller

Zollo

Zori

Zouch

Zuiker

Zumwalt

Zurcher

Zurich

Zylstra

GEOGRAPHICAL AREA

Don't discount your character's geographical location. The stage where your character lives, walks, thinks, and behaves can be an integral part of your story. It can add mood, tension, and motivation.

There are various ways a writer can use a geographical setting. The country, river, amusement park, or city can be considered a character and also an antagonist. Your protagonist can be thrown overboard into the ocean or sea, or fall into a river filled with crocodiles. Or your character, terrified of crowds, is coerced into traveling to Times Square in New York City during New Year's Eve. Locations can be endless: battling the desert without water, being cornered by wolves in Yellowstone National Park, and on and on.

Be aware, though, a geographic setting can be a cliché: a shipboard romance, or a car chase in the middle of a metropolitan city. Try to write the unexpected. What about your protagonist trapped in a historic church in Rome with a killer? Surprise the readers. Having your character placed in an unfamiliar geographical region adds tension and suspense. Imagine having your protagonist in Botswana or visiting the Great Wall of China yet only knowing English. Add more conflict by having your character lose his passport and money. You can ratchet up the tension by adding a timetable where the protagonist must get out of the country within twenty-four hours.

Setting can also create symbolism or internal conflict. A person doubting his marriage and relationship walks along an empty beach filled with trash and dead fish. A character, afraid of intimacy all his life, is now lost in the Zion National Park, alone and near death, aware no one will grieve for his passing. Or a person craving human contact after the loss of her spouse or parent finds herself walking in the crowds of the Iowa State Fair, where laughter, children and intact families are all around her.

When it comes to traveling to distant lands, do your research. Don't just drop your characters into a country, state, or city you do not know anything about. Be aware, readers will quickly call you out on what you aren't familiar with and don't research.

The lists we've compiled break down into popular destinations and cities, bodies of water, countries, U.S. states, and more. Have fun with it. Do something different!

LAND

CONTINENTS

Africa
Antarctica
Asia
Australia

Europe
North America
South America

WORLD COUNTRIES

Names, geographical, and political boundaries can change

Afghanistan
Albania
Algeria
Andorra
Angola
Antigua and Barbuda
Argentina
Armenia
Australia
Austria
Azerbaijan
Bahamas
Bahrain
Bangladesh
Barbados
Belarus
Belgium
Belize

Benin
Bhutan
Bolivia
Bosnia and Herzegovina
Botswana
Brazil
Brunei
Bulgaria
Burkina Faso
Burma
Burundi
Cabo Verde
Cambodia
Cameroon
Canada
Cayman Islands
Central African Republic
Chad

Chile

China

Colombia

Comoros

Congo, Democratic Republic of the

Congo, Republic of the

Costa Rica

Cote D'Ivoire (Ivory Coast)

Croatia

Cuba

Cyprus

Czechia

Denmark

Djibouti

Dominica

Dominican Republic

Ecuador

Egypt

El Salvador

Equatorial Guinea

Eritrea

Estonia

Eswatini

Ethiopia

Fiji

Finland

France

Gabon

Gambia

Georgia

Germany

Ghana

Greece

Grenada

Guatemala

Guinea

Guinea-Bissau

Guyana

Haiti

Honduras

Hungary

Iceland

India

Indonesia

Iran

Iraq

Ireland

Israel

Italy

Jamaica

Japan

Jordan

Kazakhstan

Kenya

Kiribati

Kosovo

Kuwait

Kyrgyzstan

Laos

Latvia

Lebanon

Lesotho

Liberia

Libya

Liechtenstein

Lithuania

Luxembourg

Macedonia

Madagascar

Malawi

Malaysia

Maldives

Mali

Malta

Marshall Islands

Mauritania

Mauritius

Mexico

Micronesia

Moldova

Monaco

Mongolia

Montenegro

Morocco

Mozambique

Myanmar (Form. Burma)

Namibia

Nauru

Nepal

Netherlands

New Zealand

Nicaragua

Niger

Nigeria

Norway

Oman

Pakistan

Palau

Panama

Papua New Guinea

Paraguay

Peoples Rep. of Korea (North Korea)

Peru

Philippines

Poland

Portugal

Qatar

Republic of Korea (South Korea)

Romania

Russia

Rwanda

Saint Kitts and Nevis

Saint Lucia

Saint Vincent and the Grenadines

Samoa

San Marino

Sao Tome and Principe

Saudi Arabia

Senegal

Serbia

Seychelles

Sierra Leone

Singapore

Slovakia

Slovenia

Solomon Islands

Somalia

South Africa

South Sudan

Spain

Sri Lanka

Sudan

Suriname

Sweden

Switzerland

Syria

Taiwan
Tajikistan
Tanzania
Thailand
Timor-Leste
Togo
Tonga
Trinidad and Tobago
Tunisia
Turkey
Turkmenistan
Tuvalu
Uganda

Ukraine
United Arab Emirates
United Kingdom
United States of America
Uruguay
Uzbekistan
Vanuatu
Vatican City
Venezuela
Vietnam
Yemen
Zambia
Zimbabwe

TERRITORY AND SPECIAL REGIONS

*Names, geographical, and political boundaries can change

Akrotiri, Territory of U.K.
American Samoa, U.S. Territory
Anguilla, U.K. Territory
Antarctica
Aruba, Netherlands Territory
Ashmore/Cartier Islands, Au. Terr.
Baker Island, U.S. Territory
Bermuda, U.K. Territory

Bouvet Island, Norway Territory
British Virgin Islands, U.K. Terr.
Christmas Island, Au. Terr.
Clipperton Island, French Territory
Cocos Islands, Australian Territory
Cook Island, Australian Territory
Coral Sea Islands, Australian Terr.
Curacao

WORLD POPULAR CITIES

Abu Dhabi, United Arab Emirates
Amman, Jordan
Antalya, Turkey
Amsterdam, Netherlands
Athens, Greece
Bangkok, Thailand

Barcelona, Spain
Beijing, China
Berlin, Germany
Brussels, Belgium
Bucharest, Romania
Budapest, Hungary

Buenos Aires, Argentina
Cairo, Egypt
Cancun, Mexico
Cape Town Central, South Africa
Chennai, India
Copenhagen, Denmark
Cusco, Peru
Dammam, Saudi Arabia
Delhi, India
Denpasar, Indonesia
Doha, Qatar
Dubai, United Arab Emirates
Dublin, Ireland
Florence, Italy
Frankfurt, Germany
Giza, Egypt
Goreme, Turkey
Hanoi, Vietnam
Ho Chi Minh City, Vietnam
Hong Kong, China
Istanbul, Turkey
Jakarta, Indonesia
Jaipur, India
Johannesburg, South Africa
Kathmandu, Nepal
Kiev, Ukraine
Krakow, Poland
Kuala Lumpur, Malaysia
Lima, Peru
Lisbon, Portugal
London, United Kingdom
Los Angeles, United States
Macau, China
Madrid, Spain

Manama, Bahrain
Manila, Philippines
Marrakech, Morocco
Mecca, Saudi Arabia
Melbourne, Australia
Mexico City, Mexico
Milan, Italy
Montreal, Canada
Moscow, Russia
Mumbai, India
Munich, Germany
Nairobi, Kenya
Nassau, Bahamas
New York City, United States
Osaka, Japan
Paris, France
Phuket, Thailand
Prague, Czech Republic
Punta Cana, Dominican Republic
Queenstown, New Zealand
Rio de Janeiro, Brazil
Rome, Italy
Seoul, South Korea
Shanghai, China
Shenzhen, China
Siem Reap, Cambodia
Singapore, Singapore
Sofia, Bulgaria
St. Petersburg, Russia
Sydney, Australia
Taipei, Taiwan
Tokyo, Japan
Toronto, Canada
Ubud, Indonesia

Vancouver, Canada
Venice, Italy
Vienna, Austria

Warsaw, Poland
Zermatt, Switzerland
Zurich, Switzerland

U.S. STATES

Alabama
Alaska
Arizona
Arkansas
California
Colorado
Connecticut
Delaware
Florida
Georgia
Hawaii
Idaho
Illinois
Indiana
Iowa
Kansas
Kentucky
Louisiana
Maine
Maryland
Massachusetts
Michigan
Minnesota
Mississippi
Missouri

Montana
Nebraska
Nevada
New Hampshire
New Jersey
New Mexico
New York
North Carolina
North Dakota
Ohio
Oklahoma
Oregon
Pennsylvania
Rhode Island
South Carolina
South Dakota
Tennessee
Texas
Utah
Vermont
Virginia
Washington
West Virginia
Wisconsin
Wyoming

U. S. STATE CAPITALS

Montgomery, AL

Juneau, AK

Phoenix, AZ

Little Rock, AR

Sacramento, CA

Denver, CO

Hartford, CT

Dover, DE

Tallahassee, FL

Atlanta, GA

Honolulu, HI

Boise, ID

Springfield, IL

Indianapolis, IN

Des Moines, IA

Topeka, KS

Frankfort, KY

Baton Rouge, LA

Augusta, ME

Annapolis, MD

Boston, MA

Lansing, MI

Saint Paul, MN

Jackson, MS

Jefferson City, MO

Helena, MT

Lincoln, NE

Carson City, NV

Concord, NH

Trenton, NJ

Santa Fe, NM

Albany, NY

Raleigh, SC

Bismarck, ND

Columbus, OH

Oklahoma City, OK

Salem, OR

Harrisburg, PA

Providence, RI

Columbia, SC

Pierre, SD

Nashville, TN

Austin, TX

Salt Lake City, UT

Montpelier, VT

Richmond, VA

Olympia, WA

Charleston, WV

Madison, WI

Cheyenne, WY

U.S. POPULAR CITIES

Anaheim, CA

Atlanta, GA

Austin, TX

Baltimore, MD

Boston, MA

Branson, MO

Charleston, SC
Charlotte, NC
Chicago, IL
Dallas, TX
Daytona Beach, FL
Denver, CO
Detroit, MI
Fort Lauderdale, FL
Honolulu, HI
Houston, TX
Indianapolis, IN
Kansas City, KS
Lahaina, HI
Las Vegas, NV
Los Angeles, CA
Miami Beach, FL
Minneapolis-Saint Paul, MN
Nashville, TN

New Orleans, LA
New York City, NY
Orlando, FL
Palm Springs, CA
Philadelphia, PA
Phoenix, AZ
Portland, OR
Saint Augustine, FL
San Antonio, TX
San Diego, CA
San Francisco, CA
Savannah, GA
Seattle, WA
Sedona, AZ
St. Louis, MO
Tampa, FL
Washington, D.C.

BODIES OF WATER

OCEANS

Atlantic
Pacific
Indian

Arctic
Southern

SEAS

INDIAN OCEAN

Andaman Sea
Arabian Sea
Bay of Bengal
Gulf of Aden
Gulf of Oman
Laccadive Sea

Mozambique Channel
Palk Strait
Persian Gulf
Red Sea
Timor Sea

PACIFIC OCEAN

AMERICAS

Bering Sea
Chilean Sea
Grau Sea
Gulf of Alaska

Gulf of California/Sea of Cortés
Salish Sea
Sea of Chiloé

ASIA AND OCEANIA

Arafura Sea

Bali Sea

Banda Sea
Bismarck Sea
Bohai Sea
Bohol Sea
Camotes Sea
Celebes Sea
Ceram Sea
Coral Sea
East China Sea
Flores Sea
Gulf of Carpentaria
Gulf of Thailand
Halmahera Sea
Java Sea

Koro Sea
Molucca Sea
Philippine Sea
Savu Sea
Sea of Japan
Sea of Okhotsk
Seto Inland Sea
Sibuyan Sea
Solomon Sea
South China Sea
Sulu Sea
Tasman Sea
Visayan Sea
Yellow Sea

ARCTIC OCEAN

Baffin Bay
Barents Sea
Beaufort Sea
Chukchi Sea
East Siberian Sea
Greenland Sea
Hudson Bay

Hudson Strait
Kara Sea
Laptev Sea
Queen Victoria Sea
The Northwest Passages
Wandel Sea

SOUTHERN OCEAN

Amundsen Sea
Bass Strait
Bellingshausen Sea
Cooperation Sea
Cosmonauts Sea
D'Urville Sea
Davis Sea

Drake Passage
Great Australian Bight
Gulf St Vincent
Investigator Strait
King Haakon VII Sea
Lazarev Sea
Mawson Sea

Riiser-Larsen Sea
Ross Sea
Scotia Sea

Somov Sea
Spencer Gulf
Weddell Sea

ATLANTIC OCEAN

THE AMERICAS

Albemarle Sound
Argentine Sea
Block Island Sound
Buzzards Bay
Caribbean Sea
Chesapeake Bay
Davis Strait
Delaware Bay
Fishers Island Sound
Gulf of Maine
Gulf of Mexico
Gulf of St. Lawrence

Jamaica Bay
Labrador Sea
Long Island Sound
Nantucket Sound
Narragansett Bay
New York Bay
Pamlico Sound
Raritan Bay
Rhode Island Sound
Sandy Hook Bay
Vineyard Sound

EUROPE, AFRICA, AND ASIA

Baltic Sea
Bay of Biscay
Black Sea
Celtic Sea
English Channel
Gulf of Guinea
Irish Sea

Mediterranean Sea
North Sea
Norwegian Sea
Sea of Azov
Sea of Marmara
Wadden Sea

NORTHERN ISLANDS

Denmark Strait   Irish Sea
Inner Seas off WC of Scotland   Irminger Sea

WONDERS OF THE WORLD

7 NATURAL WONDERS
OF THE WORLD

Grand Canyon
Harbour of Rio de Janeiro, Brazil
Parícutin Volcano, Mexico
Northern Lights
Victoria Falls, Zambia/Zimbabwe
Great Barrier Reef, Australia
Mount Everest, Nepal

7 MAN-MADE WONDERS
OF THE WORLD

Great Wall of China, China
Machu Picchu, Cuzco, Peru
Petra, Wadi Musa, Jordan
Taj Mahal, Agra, India
The Colosseum, Rome, Italy
Christ the Redeemer, Brazil
Chíchen Itzá, Yucatan, Mexico

7 ANCIENT MAN-MADE WONDERS
OF THE WORLD

Great Pyramid of Giza, Egypt
Colossus of Rhodes
Hanging Gardens of Babylon

Lighthouse of Alexandria, Egypt.
Mausoleum at Halicarnassus, Turkey.
Statue of Zeus at Olympia, Greece.
Temple of Artemis at Ephesus, Turkey

POPULAR DESTINATIONS

POPULAR WORLD DESTINATIONS

Acropolis, Greece
Amsterdam, Netherlands,
Anakena Beach, Easter Island
Angel Falls, Venezuela
Angkor Wat, Cambodia
Anne Frank House, Netherlands
Athens, Greece
Auschwitz Memorial, Germany
Ayutthaya, Thailand
Bagan, Myanmar
Banff, Alberta
Barcelona, Spain
Bay Islands, Honduras
Bay of Fundy, N.B., Canada
Berlin Wall, Germany
Big Ben, London
Blarney Castle, Ireland
Blue Mosque, Istanbul
Bonaire Marine Park, Lesser Antilles
Bora Bora
Buddha at Kamakura, Japan
Cairo, Egypt
Cambridge, England
Château Frontenac, Canada
Chichen Itza, Mexico
CN Tower, Toronto Canada

Costa Rica
Count Dracula's Castle, Romania
Cristo Redentor, Brazil
Dead Sea, Israel; Jordan; West Bank
Dubai, United Arab Emirates
Easter Island, Chili
Edinburgh Castle, Scotland
Eiffel Tower, France
Fiordland National Park, New Zealand
Florence, Italy
Forbidden City, Beijing, China
Galápagos Islands, Ecuador
Ganges River in Varanasi
Genocide Memorial, Kigali, Rwanda
Golden Temple, India
Great Barrier Reef
Hanoi's Old Quarter, Vietnam
Hasan II Mosque, Casablanca
Havana, Cuba
Hiroshima, Japan
Iguazu Falls, Argentina/Brazil
Kakadu National Park, Australia
Kjeragbolten, Norway
Ko Tao, Thailand
Kong Family Mansion, Qufu, China
La Sagrada Familia, Spain

Lake Baikal, Russia
Lake Bled,
Loch Ness, Scotland
Louvre Museum, France
Machu Picchu, Peru
Marrakech, Morocco
Masai Mara, Kenya
Matterhorn, Switzerland
Millau Bridge, France
Mount Everest, Nepal, China
Mount Fuji, Japan
Mount Kilimanjaro, Tanzania
Mt. Fuji, Japan
Naqsh-E Jahan, Iran
Ngorongoro Crater, Tanzania
Oktoberfest, Germany
Old Town Square, Czech Republic
Palace of Versailles, France
Panama Canal, Panama
Paris, France
Paro Taktsang, Bhutan
Piazza San Marco, Italy
Pompeii, Italy
Prague, Czech Republic

Red Square, Moscow
Rio de Janeiro, Brazil
Rock of Gibraltar
Rome, Italy
Salar De Uyuni, Bolivia
Salisbury Cathedral, England
Socotra, Yemen
St. Basil's Cathedral, Russia
St. Peter's Basilica, Vatican
Stonehenge, England
Sydney, Australia
Tahiti
Taj Mahal, India
Temple of Confucius, China
The Amazon Rainforest
The Leaning Tower of Pisa, Italy
The Pyramids of Giza, Egypt
Tianzi Mountains, China
Tiger Leaping Gorge, China
Twelve Apostles, Australia
Valley of the Kings, Egypt
Venice, Italy
Vienna, Austria
Western (Wailing) Wall, Jerusalem

POPULAR U.S. DESTINATIONS

9/11 Memorial & Museum, NY
Acadia National Park, MN
Alcatraz Island, San Francisco, CA
Antelope Canyon, AZ
Apostle Islands, WI
Arlington National Cemetery, VA
Avery Island, LA

Big Sur, CA
Biltmore Estate, NC
Boundary Waters, MN
Bourbon Street, New Orleans, LA
Bryce Canyon National Park, UT
Cannon Beach, OR
Cape Flattery, WA

Carlsbad Caverns, NM
Central Park, NY
Charleston, SC
Chinatown, San Francisco, CA
Crater Lake National Park, OR
Diamond Head Monument, HI
Disneyland, CA
Disneyworld, FL
Dry Tortugas National Park, FL
Empire State Building, NY
Epcot Center, FL
Everglades National Park, FL
Fenway Park, Boston, MA
Florida Keys, FL
Four Corners
Freedom Trail, Boston, MA
French Quarter, LA
Garden of the Gods, CO
Gateway Arch, St. Louis, MO
Gila Cliff Dwellings, NM
Glacier National Park, MT
Golden Gate Bridge, CA
Graceland, TN
Grand Canyon, AZ
Grand Central Terminal, NY
Grand Ole Opry, TN
Grand Prismatic Spring, WY
Grand Teton National Park, WY
Great Smoky Mountains, TN
Grotto of the Redemption, IO
Hearst Castle, CA
Hollywood sign/Sunset Strip, CA
Horseshoe Bend, AZ
Hot Springs, AR

Independence Square, MO
Iowa State Fair, IA
Joshua Tree National Park, CA
Kennedy Space Center, FL
Liberty Bell, Philadelphia, PA
Library of Congress, D.C.
Martha's Vineyard, MA
Mesa Verde National Park, CO
Millennium Park, IL
Monument Valley, UT
Mount Rushmore, SD
Multnomah Falls, OR
Mutual of Omaha Zoo, NE
Nantucket/Martha's Vineyard, MA
Napa Valley, CA
Nāpali Coastline, HI
Nashville, TN
Northern Lights, AK
Pacific Coast Highway, CA
Pike Place Market, WA
Plymouth Rock, MA
Powell's Bookstore, Portland, OR
Quechee Gorge State Park, VT
Redwood National Park, CA
Rocky Mountain National Park
Roswell, NM
Saguaro National Park, AZ
Salem Witch Museum, MA
San Antonio Missions, TX
San Diego Zoo, CA
San Francisco, CA
San Xavier Mission, AZ
Santa Fe, NM
Sedona, AZ

Sisters of St. Benedict Monastery, IN

Smithsonian and Space Museum, D.C

South Beach, Miami, FL

Space Center, Houston, TX

Space Needle, Seattle, WA

Statue of Liberty, NY

Stratosphere Tower, NV

Taos Pueblo, NM

The Alamo, TX

The Breakers, RI

The Narrows, Zion National Park. UT

The USS Arizona Memorial, HI

The Wave, Vermillion Cliffs, AZ

Thomas Jefferson Memorial, D.C.

Times Square, NY

Venice Beach/Santa Monica Pier, CA

White House, Washington D.C.

White Sands, NM

Wrigley Field, IL

Yellowstone National Park

Yosemite National Forest, CA

Zion National Park, UT

ANIMALS

Want to take a leap into a different territory and have an animal as one of your characters? Maybe a Pekingese or a platypus? Or you're just not sure what? The lists below break down hundreds of animals from domestic and wild to birds, insects, and fish. You can decide to have a realistic animal or one that talks and acts like a human. *Charlotte's Web, Black Beauty,* and *Watership Down* are a few examples of animals with human characteristics. Stories with animals as the main characters are usually about us, able to create empathy and portray family dynamics and friendships. Having animals with human traits can also convey a multitude of emotions, from love and betrayal to grief and joy.

Delve into what makes an animal a dog, cat, horse, zebra or turkey. Just like humans, an animal has motives and certain characteristics. Readers will find a mouse chasing a dog unrealistic, unless you give a motivation behind that animal's actions. Blending in backstory for the animal will also help a reader identify with the animal. We all know pigs don't fly, but if you give enough characterization, motives, and the right setting, you can suspend a reader's disbelief and have him seduced into believing anything.

Even if you only intend to have animals in your story as minor focal points, the lists below can help you drill down to a specific breed. If you are planning to include a realistic animal, don't forget to do your research. You can't have an herbivore eating meat. Also, animals do have distinct personalities, so you can play that up.

Not sure what animal you want to add to a scene or story? Stuck on your run-of-the-mill domesticated golden retriever? The lists we've compiled will be sure to spark your imagination or give you ideas as to what direction you would like to go.

DOMESTICATED

DOGS

Affenpinscher
Afghan Hound
Afghan Shepherd
Aidi
Airedale Terrier
Akbash
Akita
Alano Español
Alaskan Husky
Alaskan Klee Kai
Alaskan Malamute
Alaunt
Alopekis
Alpine Dachsbracke
Alpine Mastiff
Alpine Spaniel
American Akita
American Bulldog
American Cocker Spaniel
American English Coonhound
American Eskimo Dog
American Foxhound
American Hairless Terrier
American Pit Bull Terrier
American Staffordshire Terrier
American Water Spaniel
Anatolian Shepherd Dog

Andalusian Hound
Anglo-Français de Petite Vénerie
Appenzeller Sennenhund
Ariegeois
Armant
Armenian Gampr dog
Artois Hound
Australian Cattle Dog
Australian Kelpie
Australian Shepherd
Australian Silky Terrier
Australian Stumpy Tail Cattle Dog
Australian Terrier
Austrian Black and Tan Hound
Austrian Pinscher
Azawakh
Bakharwal dog
Barbet
Basenji
Basque Shepherd Dog
Basset Artésien Normand
Basset Bleu de Gascogne
Basset Fauve de Bretagne
Basset Hound
Bavarian Mountain Hound
Beagle
Beagle-Harrier

Bearded Collie

Beauceron

Bedlington Terrier

Belgian Shepherd Dog (Groenendael)

Belgian Shepherd Dog (Laekenois)

Belgian Shepherd Dog (Malinois)

Belgian Shepherd Dog (Tervuren)

Bergamasco Shepherd

Berger Blanc Suisse

Berger Picard

Bernese Mountain Dog

Bichon Frisé

Billy

Black and Tan Coonhound

Black and Tan Virginia Foxhound

Black Mouth Cur

Black Norwegian Elkhound

Black Russian Terrier

Bloodhound

Blue Heeler

Blue Lacy

Blue Paul Terrier

Blue Picardy Spaniel

Bluetick Coonhound

Boerboel

Bohemian Shepherd

Bolognese

Border Collie

Border Terrier

Borzoi

Bosnian Coarse-haired Hound

Boston Terrier

Bouvier des Ardennes

Bouvier des Flandres

Boxer

Boykin Spaniel

Bracco Italiano

Braque d'Auvergne

Braque de l'Ariege

Braque du Bourbonnais

Braque du Puy

Braque Francais

Braque Saint-Germain

Brazilian Dogo

Brazilian Terrier

Briard

Briquet Griffon Vendéen

Brittany

Broholmer

Bruno Jura Hound

Bucovina Shepherd Dog

Bull and Terrier

Bull Terrier

Bulldog

Bullenbeisser

Bullmastiff

Bully Kutta

Burgos Pointer

Cairn Terrier

Canaan Dog

Canadian Eskimo Dog

Cane Corso

Cantabrian Water Dog

Cão da Serra de Aires

Cão de Castro Laboreiro

Cão de Gado Transmontano

Cão Fila de São Miguel

Carolina Dog

Carpathian Shepherd Dog
Catahoula Leopard Dog
Catalan Sheepdog
Caucasian Shepherd Dog
Cavalier King Charles Spaniel
Central Asian Shepherd Dog
Cesky Fousek
Cesky Terrier
Chesapeake Bay Retriever
Chien Français Blanc et Noir
Chien Français Blanc et Orange
Chien Français Tricolor
Chien-gris
Chihuahua
Chilean Fox Terrier
Chinese Chongqing Dog
Chinese Crested Dog
Chinese Imperial Dog
Chinook
Chippiparai
Chow Chow
Cierny Sery
Cimarrón Uruguayo
Cirneco dell'Etna
Clumber Spaniel
Collie, Rough
Collie, Smooth
Combai
Cordoba Fighting Dog
Coton de Tulear
Cretan Hound
Croatian Sheepdog
Cumberland Sheepdog
Curly-Coated Retriever

Cursinu
Czechoslovakian Wolfdog
Dachshund
Dalmatian
Dandie Dinmont Terrier
Danish-Swedish Farmdog
Deutsche Bracke
Doberman Pinscher
Dogo Argentino
Dogo Cubano
Dogue de Bordeaux
Drentse Patrijshond
Drever
Dunker
Dutch Shepherd
Dutch Smoushond
East European Shepherd
East Siberian Laika
Elo
English Cocker Spaniel
English Foxhound
English Setter
English Shepherd
English Springer Spaniel
English Toy Terrier (Black & Tan)
English Water Spaniel
English White Terrier
Entlebucher Mountain Dog
Estonian Hound
Estrela Mountain Dog
Eurasier
Eurohound
Field Spaniel
Fila Brasileiro

Finnish Hound
Finnish Lapphund
Finnish Spitz
Flat-Coated Retriever
Fox Terrier, Smooth
Fox Terrier, Wire
French Brittany
French Bulldog
French Spaniel
Gaddi Dog
Galgo Español
Galician Cattle Dog
Garafian Shepherd
Gascon Saintongeois
Georgian Shepherd Dog
German Longhaired Pointer
German Pinscher
German Roughhaired Pointer
German Shepherd Dog
German Shorthaired Pointer
German Spaniel
German Spitz
German Wirehaired Pointer
Giant Schnauzer
Glen of Imaal Terrier
Golden Retriever
Gordon Setter
Gran Mastín de Borínquen
Grand Anglo-Français Blanc et Noir
Grand Anglo-Français Blanc et Orange
Grand Anglo-Français Tricolore
Grand Basset Griffon Vendéen
Grand Bleu de Gascogne
Grand Griffon Vendéen

Great Dane
Great Pyrenees
Greater Swiss Mountain Dog
Greek Harehound
Greenland Dog
Greyhound
Griffon Bleu de Gascogne
Griffon Bruxellois
Griffon Fauve de Bretagne
Griffon Nivernais
Guatemalan Dogo
Hamiltonstövare
Hanover Hound
Hare Indian Dog
Harrier
Havanese
Hawaiian Poi Dog
Himalayan Sheepdog
Hokkaido
Hortaya Borzaya
Hovawart
Huntaway
Hygenhund
Ibizan Hound
Icelandic Sheepdog
Indian pariah dog
Indian Spitz
Irish Red and White Setter
Irish Setter
Irish Terrier
Irish Water Spaniel
Irish Wolfhound
Istrian Coarse-haired Hound
Istrian Shorthaired Hound

Italian Greyhound

Jack Russell Terrier

Jagdterrier

Jämthund

Japanese Chin

Japanese Spitz

Japanese Terrier

Kai Ken

Kaikadi

Kangal Dog

Kanni

Karakachan Dog

Karelian Bear Dog

Karst Shepherd

Keeshond

Kerry Beagle

Kerry Blue Terrier

King Charles Spaniel

King Shepherd

Kintamani

Kishu Ken

Komondor

Kooikerhondje

Koolie

Korean Jindo

Kromfohrländer

Kumaon Mastiff

Kunming Wolfdog

Kurī

Kuvasz

Kyi-Leo

Labrador Husky

Labrador Retriever

Lagotto Romagnolo

Lakeland Terrier

Lancashire Heeler

Landseer

Lapponian Herder

Leonberger

Lhasa Apso

Lithuanian Hound

Löwchen

Mackenzie River Husky

Magyar Agár

Mahratta Greyhound

Majorca Ratter

Majorca Shepherd Dog

Maltese

Manchester Terrier

Maremma Sheepdog

Mastiff

McNab

Mexican Hairless Dog

Miniature American Shepherd

Miniature Australian Shepherd

Miniature Bull Terrier

Miniature Fox Terrier

Miniature Pinscher

Miniature Schnauzer

Miniature Shar Pei

Molossus

Molossus of Epirus

Montenegrin Mountain Hound

Moscow Watchdog

Moscow Water Dog

Mountain Cur

Mucuchies

Mudhol Hound

Mudi
Münsterländer, Large
Münsterländer, Small
Neapolitan Mastiff
New Zealand Heading Dog
Newfoundland
Norfolk Spaniel
Norfolk Terrier
Norrbottenspets
North Country Beagle
Northern Inuit Dog
Norwegian Buhund
Norwegian Elkhound
Norwegian Lundehund
Norwich Terrier
Nova Scotia Duck Tolling Retriever
Old Croatian Sighthound
Old Danish Pointer
Old English Bulldog
Old English Sheepdog
Old English Terrier
Old German Shepherd Dog
Old Time Farm Shepherd
Olde English Bulldogge
Otterhound
Pachon Navarro
Paisley Terrier
Pandikona Hunting Dog
Papillon
Parson Russell Terrier
Patterdale Terrier
Pekingese
Perro de Presa Canario
Perro de Presa Mallorquin

Peruvian Hairless Dog
Petit Basset Griffon Vendéen
Petit Bleu de Gascogne
Phalène
Pharaoh Hound
Phu Quoc Ridgeback
Picardy Spaniel
Plott Hound
Plummer Terrier
Podenco Canario
Pointer
Poitevin
Polish Greyhound
Polish Hound
Polish Hunting Dog
Polish Lowland Sheepdog
Polish Tatra Sheepdog
Pomeranian
Pont-Audemer Spaniel
Poodle
Porcelaine
Portuguese Podengo
Portuguese Pointer
Portuguese Water Dog
Posavac Hound
Pražský Krysařík
Pudelpointer
Pug
Puli
Pumi
Pungsan Dog
Pyrenean Mastiff
Pyrenean Shepherd
Rafeiro do Alentejo

Rajapalayam
Rampur Greyhound
Rastreador Brasileiro
Rat Terrier
Ratonero Bodeguero Andaluz
Ratonero Murciano de Huerta
Ratonero Valenciano
Redbone Coonhound
Rhodesian Ridgeback
Romanian Mioritic Shepherd Dog
Rottweiler
Russell Terrier
Russian Spaniel
Russian Toy
Russian Tracker
Russo-European Laika
Saarloos Wolfdog
Sabueso Español
Sabueso fino Colombiano
Saint-Usuge Spaniel
Sakhalin Husky
Saluki
Samoyed
Sapsali
Šarplaninac
Schapendoes
Schillerstövare
Schipperke
Schweizer Laufhund
Schweizerischer Niederlaufhund
Scotch Collie
Scottish Deerhound
Scottish Terrier
Sealyham Terrier

Segugio Italiano
Seppala Siberian Sleddog
Serbian Hound
Serbian Tricolour Hound
Seskar Seal Dog
Shar Pei
Shetland Sheepdog
Shiba Inu
Shih Tzu
Shikoku
Shiloh Shepherd
Siberian Husky
Silken Windhound
Sinhala Hound
Skye Terrier
Sloughi
Slovak Cuvac
Slovakian Wirehaired Pointer
Slovenský Kopov
Smålandsstövare
Small Greek Domestic Dog
Soft-Coated Wheaten Terrier
South Russian Ovcharka
Southern Hound
Spanish Mastiff
Spanish Water Dog
Spinone Italiano
Sporting Lucas Terrier
St. Bernard
St. John's Water Dog
Stabyhoun
Staffordshire Bull Terrier
Standard Schnauzer
Stephens Cur

Styrian Coarse-haired Hound
Sussex Spaniel
Swedish Lapphund
Swedish Vallhund
Tahltan Bear Dog
Taigan
Taiwan Dog
Talbot
Tamaskan Dog
Teddy Roosevelt Terrier
Telomian
Tenterfield Terrier
Terceira Mastiff
Thai Bangkaew Dog
Thai Ridgeback
Tibetan Mastiff
Tibetan Spaniel
Tibetan Terrier
Tornjak
Tosa
Toy Bulldog
Toy Fox Terrier
Toy Manchester Terrier
Toy Trawler Spaniel
Transylvanian Hound
Treeing Cur
Treeing Tennessee Brindle

Treeing Walker Coonhound
Trigg Hound
Tweed Water Spaniel
Tyrolean Hound
Valencian Ratter
Vanjari Hound
Villano de Las Encartaciones
Villanuco de Las Encartaciones
Vizsla
Volpino Italiano
Weimaraner
Welsh Corgi, Cardigan
Welsh Corgi, Pembroke
Welsh Sheepdog
Welsh Springer Spaniel
Welsh Terrier
West Highland White Terrier
West Siberian Laika
Westphalian Dachsbracke
Wetterhoun
Whippet
White Shepherd
Wirehaired Pointing Griffon
Wirehaired Vizsla
Xiasi Dog
Yorkshire Terrier

CATS

Abyssinian
Aegean
American Bobtail
American Curl

American Shorthair
American Wirehair
Aphrodite Giant
Arabian Mau

Asian
Asian Semi-longhair
Australian Mist
Balinese
Bambino
Bengal
Birman
Bombay
Brazilian Shorthair
British Longhair
British Semi-longhair
British Shorthair
Burmese
Burmilla
California Spangled
Chantilly-Tiffany
Chartreux
Chausie
Cheetoh
Colorpoint Shorthair
Cornish Rex
Cymric, or Longhaired Manx
Cyprus
Devon Rex
Donskoy, or Don Sphynx
Dragon Li
Dwelf
Egyptian Mau
European Shorthair
Exotic Shorthair
Foldex
German Rex
Havana Brown
Highlander

Himalayan, or Colorpoint Persian
Japanese Bobtail
Javanese, or Colorpoint Longhair
Karelian Bobtail
Khao Manee
Korat
Korean Bobtail
Korn Ja
Kurilian or Kuril Islands Bobtail
LaPerm
Lykoi
Maine Coon
Manx
Mekong Bobtail
Minskin
Munchkin
Napoleon
Nebelung
Norwegian Forest cat
Ocicat
Ojos Azules
Oregon Rex
Oriental Bicolor
Oriental Longhair
Oriental Shorthair
Persian (modern)
Persian (traditional)
Peterbald
Pixie-bob
Raas
Ragamuffin, or Liebling
Ragdoll
Russian Blue
Russian White, Black, and Tabby

Sam Sawet
Savannah
Scottish Fold
Selkirk Rex
Serengeti
Serrade petit
Siamese
Siberian, or Siberian Forest Cat
Singapura
Snowshoe
Sokoke
Somali

Sphynx
Suphalak
Thai Lilac
Thai, or Traditional, Classic
Tonkinese
Toyger
Turkish Angora
Turkish Van
Ukrainian Levkoy
Wila Krungthep
York Chocolate

PET BIRDS

Canary—American Singer
Canary—Australian Plainhead
Canary—Belgium
Canary—Black-headed
Canary—Border
Canary—Cinnamon
Canary—Crested
Canary—Fife
Canary—Frilled
Canary—German Roller
Canary—Gloster
Canary—Lancashire
Canary—Lizard
Canary—Norwich
Canary—Parisian Frill
Canary—Red Factor
Canary—Roller
Canary—Scottish
Canary—Spanish Timbrado

Canary—Stafford
Canary—Waterslager
Canary—Yellow-fronted
Canary—Yorkshire
Cockatiel—Cinnamon
Cockatiel—Lutino
Cockatiel—Normal Grey
Cockatiel—Pearl
Cockatiel—Pied
Cockatiel—Whiteface
Cockatoo
Cockatoo—Bare-eyed
Cockatoo—Sulphur Crested
Cockatoo—Rose Breasted
Conure—Blue Crown
Conure—Golden
Conure—Jenday
Conure—Sun
Conure—Green-cheeked

Dove—Band-tailed Pigeon
Dove—Common Ground
Dove—Eurasian Collared Dove
Dove—Inca
Dove—Mourning
Dove—Rock Dove (Rock Pigeon)
Dove—White-tipped
Dove—White-winged
Finch—'Apapane
Finch—American Goldfinch
Finch—Azores Bullfinch
Finch—Black Siskin
Finch—Brambling
Finch—Carduelis
Finch—Common
Finch—Common Redpoll
Finch—Common Rosefinch
Finch—Crimson-browed
Finch—Crossbills
Finch—Desert
Finch—Eurasian Bullfinch
Finch—Eurasian Siskin
Finch—European Gold
Finch—European Greenfinch
Finch—Evening
Finch—Gray-crowned Rosy Finch
Finch—Grey-capped Greenfinch
Finch—Hawaiian Honeycreeper
Finch—Hawfinch
Finch—Hooded Sisken
Finch—House
Finch—Japanese Grosbeak
Finch—Lawrence's Goldfinch
Finch—Lesser Goldfinch

Finch—Mountain Serin
Finch—Pine
Finch—Pine Grosbeak
Finch—Po'ouli
Finch—Purple
Finch—Pyrrhula
Finch—Red crossbill
Finch—Red Sisken
Finch—Rosefinch
Finch—Serinus
Finch—Tenerife Blue Chaffinch
Finch—Zebra
Lorikeet—Black-capped
Lorikeet—Black-winged
Lorikeet—Coconut
Lorikeet—Musk
Lorikeet—Papuan
Lorikeet—Pohnpei
Lorikeet—Rainbow
Lorikeet—Red-collared
Lorikeet—Scaly-breasted
Lorikeet—Yellow-backed
Lory—Black-capped
Lory—Chattering
Lory—Purple-bellied
Lory—Purple-naped
Lory—Red
Lory—White-naped
Lory—Yellow-bibbed
Lovebird—Black-cheeked
Lovebird—Black-collared
Lovebird—Black-winged
Lovebird—Fischer's
Lovebird—Grey-headed

Lovebird—Lilian's (Nyasa)

Lovebird—Peach-faced

Lovebird—Red-headed (Red-faced)

Lovebird—Yellow-collared

Macaw—Blue and Gold

Macaw—Blue-winged

Macaw—Blue-throated

Macaw—Chestnut-fronted

Macaw—Cuban

Macaw—Glaucous

Macaw—Golden-collared

Macaw—Great Green

Macaw—Greenwing

Macaw—hybrid

Macaw—Lear's

Macaw—Lesser Antillean

Macaw—Military

Macaw—Red and Green

Macaw—Red-bellied

Macaw—Red-shouldered

Macaw—Scarlet

Macaw—Spix's

Macaw—Yyacinth

Parakeet—Alexandrine

Parakeet—Australian

Parakeet—Brotogeris

Parakeet—Golden

Parakeet—Horned

Parakeet—Indian Ringneck

Parakeet—Lineolated

Parakeet—Monk

Parakeet—Opaline

Parakeet—Pink

Parakeet—Plum-headed

Parakeet—Psittacula

Parakeet—Purple

Parakeet—Rainbow Spangle

Parakeet—Ring-necked

Parakeet—Rose-ringed

Parakeet—Sparkle

Parakeet—Whipper

Parrot—African Grey

Parrot—Amazon

Parrot—Australian King

Parrot—Black-headed

Parrot—Bronze-winged

Parrot—Crimson Rosella

Parrot—Dusky Ivory

Parrot—Eastern Rosella

Parrot—Eclectus

Parrot—Lilac-crowned

Parrot—Lophochroa Leadbeateri

Parrot—Pionus

Parrot—Princess

Parrot—Quaker

Parrot—Red-capped

Parrot—Western Rosella

Parrotlet—Blue-fronted

Parrotlet—Blue-winged

Parrotlet—Brown-backed

Parrotlet—Dusky-billed

Parrotlet—Golden-tailed

Parrotlet—Green-rumped

Parrotlet—Lilac-tailed

Parrotlet—Manu

Parrotlet—Mexican

Parrotlet—Pacific

Parrotlet—Red-fronted

Parrotlet—Sapphire-rumped

Parrotlet—Scarlet-shouldered

Parrotlet—Spectacled

Parrotlet—Spot-winged

Parrotlet—Tepui

Parrotlet—Yellow-faced

LIVESTOCK & SMALLSTOCK

HORSES

Akhal-Teke
Andalusian
Appaloosa
Arabian
Belgian
Clydesdale
Draft
Lipizzan
Miniature

Morgan
Mustang
Paint
Pony
Quarter Horse
Tennessee Walker
Thoroughbred
Warmblood

DAIRY CATTLE

American Milking Devon
Ayrshire
Brown Swiss
Buša
Canadienne
Dairy Shorthorn
Dexter
Guernsey
Holstein-Friesian

Illawarra
Irish Moiled
Jersey
Milking Shorthorn
Montbéliarde
Normande
Norwegian Red
Red Poll

BEEF CATTLE

Aberdeen Angus
Adaptaur
Afrikaner cattle

Australian Braford
Australian Brangus
Australian Charbray

Beefalo

Beefmaster

Belgian Blue

Belmont Red

Belted Galloway

Black Hereford

Blonde d'Aquitaine

Bonsmara

Boran

Brahman

Brangus

British White

Caracu

Charolais

Chianina

Corriente

Crioulo Lageano

Dexter

Droughtmaster

English Longhorn

Fleckvieh

Florida Cracker cattle

Galloway

Gascon cattle

Gelbvieh

Han-u

Hereford

Hérens

Highland

Hungarian Grey

Irish Moiled

Jabres

Limousin

Lincoln Red

Lowline

Luing

Madurese

Maine-Anjou

Mocho Nacional

Murray Grey

Nelore

Nguni

North Devon

Piedmontese

Pineywoods

Pinzgauer

Red Angus

Red Poll

Red Sindhi

Romagnola

Romosinuano

Salers

Santa Gertrudis

Shorthorn/Beef Shorthorn

Simmental

Square Meater

Sussex

Tabapuan

Tajima

Texas Longhorn

Wagyū

Welsh Black

White Park

Żubroń

GOATS

Abaza
Abergelle
Adamello blond
Afar
Agew
Agrupación de las Mesetas
Albatinah
Algarvia
Aljabal Alakhdar
Alpine
Altai Mountain
Andaman local
Anglo-Nubian
Angora
Appenzell goat
Aradi
Arapawa
Argentata dell'Etna
Arsi-Bale
Asmari
Aspromonte
Assam Hill
Aswad
Attappady Black
Attaouia
Auckland Island
Australian brown
Australian Cashmere
Australian Heritage Angora
Australian Melaan
Australian Miniature
Azpi Gorri

Azul
Bagot
Banatian White
Barbari
Beetal
Belgian Fawn
Benadir
Bhuj
Bilberry
Bionda dell'Adamello
Black Bengal
Boer
Booted
British Alpine
Brown Shorthair
Canary Island
Canindé
Carpathian
Chyangra
Chamba
Chamois Coloured
Changthangi
Chappar
Charnequeira
Chengde Polled
Chengdu Brown
Chigu
Chué
Corsican
Dera Din Panah
Damani
Damascus

Danish Landrace
Don
Duan
Dutch Landrace
Dutch Toggenburg
Erzgebirge
Fainting
Frisa Valtellinese
Finnish Landrace
Garganica
Girgentana
Göingeget
Golden Guernsey
Grisons Striped
Guddi
Hailun
Haimen
Hasi
Hejazi
Hexi Cashmere
Hongtong
Huaipi
Huaitoutala
Hungarian Improved
Icelandic
Irish
Jamnapari
Jining Grey
Jonica
Kaghani
Kalahari Red
Kalbian
Kamori
Kinder

Kiko
Korean black
Kri-kri
La Mancha
Laoshan
Majorera
Malabari
Maltese
Massif Central
Markhoz
Messinese
Mini Oberhasli
Mountain
Murcia-Granada
Murciana
Nachi
Nigerian Dwarf
Nigora
North American Cashmere
Nera Verzasca
Norwegian
Oberhasli
Orobica
Peacock
Pinzgauer
Philippine
Poitou
Pridonskaya
Pygmy
Pygora
Pyrenean
Qinshan
Red Boer
Red Mediterranean

Repartida
Rove
Russian White
Saanen
Sable Saanen
Valdostana
Sahelian
San Clemente Island
Sarda
Short-eared Somali
Sirohi
Swedish Landrace
Somali
Spanish
Stiefelgeiss
Surati

Syrian Mountain
Tauernsheck
Thuringian
Toggenburg
Uzbek Black
Valais Blackneck
Vatani
Verata
West African Dwarf
White Shorthaired
Xinjiang
Xuhai
Yemen Mountain
Zalawadi
Zhiwulin Black
Zhongwei

SHEEP

American Tunis
Awassi
Badger Face Welsh Mountain
Barbados Black Belly
Black Welsh
Border Leicester
Charollais
Cheviot
Clun Forest
Columbia
Coopworth
Corriedale
Cotswold
Delaine Merino
Dorper

Dorset Down
Dorset Horn
East Friesian
Finnsheep
Hampshire
Herdwick
Jacob
Karakul
Katahdin
Kerry Hill
Leicester Longwool
Lincoln
Merino
Navajo-Churro
Norfolk Horn

North Country Cheviot
Perendale
Polypay
Rambouillet
Romanov
Romney
Ryeland
Scottish Blackface
Shetland
Shropshire

Soay
Southdown
St. Croix
Suffolk
Targhee
Teeswater
Texel
Welsh Mountain
Wensleydale
Wiltshire Horn

CHICKENS

Ancona
Appenzeller
Araucana
Australorp
Barnevelder
Booted Bantam
Bresse
Cahntecler
Calfiornia Grey
Camprine
Cochin
Cornish
Cubalaya
Dominique
Dorking
Faiyumi
Faverolles
Frizzle
German Langshan
Hamburg
Houdan

ISA Brown
Japanese bantam
Jersey
Jersey Giant
Lakenvelder
Lamona
Leghorn
Marans
Minorca
Moderne
New Hampshire
Old English Game
Orpington
Playmouth Rock
Polish
Rhode Island Red
Rosecomb
Scots Dumpy
Sebright
Serama
Shamo

Silkie
Sultan

Sussex
Yokohama

DUCKS

American Black
American Wigeon
Barrows Goldeneye
Black Scoter
Black-bellied whistling
Blue-winged Teal
Bufflehead
Canvasback
Cinnamon Teal
Common Eider
Common Goldeneye
Common Merganser
Eurasian Wigeon
Fulvous Whistling
Gadwall
Greater Scaup
Green-winged Teal
Harlequin

Hooded
King
Lesser Scaup
Long-Tailed
Mallard
Marbled
Mottled
Northern Pintail
Northern Shoveler
Red-breasted Merganser
Redhead
Ring-necked
Ruddy
Spectacled Eider
Stellers Eider
Surf Scoter
White-winged Scoter
Wood

GEESE

Barnacle
Brant
Cackling
Canada
Emperor

Hawaiian Nene
Ross's
Snow
White-fronted

OTHER FOWL

American Coot

Mute Swan

Sandhill Crane

Tundra Swan

Trumpeter Swan

Turkey

MAMMALS IN THE WILD

AQUATIC MAMMAL

Blue whale
Dolphin
Humpback whale
Manatee
Monk seal
Orca
Otter

Porpoise
Sea lion
Seal
Sperm whale
Spinner dolphin
Walrus

CARNIVORE

Black Bear
Brown bear
Cheetah
Coyote
Fox
Giant panda
Hyena
Jaguar
Leopard
Lion
Lynx
Mountain lion

Ocelot
Panda
Panther
Polar bear
Puma
Snow leopard
Tasmanian Devil
Tiger
Wildcat/Bobcat
Wolf
Wolverine

MEDIUM/SMALL CARNIVORE

Badger
Ermine

Ferret
Meerkat

Mink
Mongoose
Polecat
Raccoon

Ringtail cat
Skunk
Weasel
Wolverine

LARGE HERBIVORE

African buffalo
Alpaca
Antelope
Bison
Buffalo
Camel
Deer
Donkey
Elephant
Elk
Gazelle
Giraffe
Goat
Hippopotamus
Horse

Jackass
Llama
Moose
Mountain goat
Mule
Mustang
Pronghorn
Reindeer
Rhinoceros
Sheep
Yak
Zebra
Zebu
Wildebeest

SMALL-MED HERBIVORES AND INSECTIVORES

Anteater
Armadillo
Bat
Capybara
Cottontail rabbit
Hare/jackrabbit

Hedgehog
Mole
Pika
Platypus
Shrew
Sloth

MARSUPIAL

Bandicoot
Kangaroo
Koala bear
Marsupial mole
Marsupial mouse
Musky rat-kangaroo

Opossum
Rat kangaroos
Tasmanian devils
Wallaby
Wallaroo
Wombat

PRIMATE

Ape
Monkey
Gorilla
Orangutan
Chimpanzee

Gibbon
Baboon
Lemur
Tamarin

RODENT

Beaver
Chinchilla
Chipmunk
Gerbil
Gopher
Groundhog
Guinea pig
Hamster
Lemming

Marmot
Mink
Mouse
Porcupine
Prairie dog
Rat
Squirrel
Woodchuck

REPTILES AND AMPHIBIANS

AMPHIBIAN—SALAMANDER

Mole
Mudpuppies

Newt
Tadpole

AMPHIBIAN—FROGS

Bullfrog
Glass/leaf
Marsupial
Painted
Poison dart
Pond

Running
Screeching
Tailed
Toad
Tree

REPTILE—LARGE

Aldabra giant tortoise
American alligator
American crocodile
Black caiman
Galapagos tortoise
Giant tortoise
Green anaconda
Green sea turtle

Komodo dragon
Leatherback sea turtle
Loggerhead sea turtle
Mugger crocodile
Nile crocodile
Orinoco crocodile
Saltwater crocodile
Slender-snouted crocodile

REPTILE—SMALL

Lizard
Iguana
Gila monster

Gecko
Chameleon

REPTILE—SNAKES

Adder

Asp

Boa

Bull

Cobra

Copperhead

Coral

Cottonmouth

Garter

Gopher

Hognose

Kingsnakes

Mamba

Python

Racer

Rat

Rattlesnake

Sea

Sidewinder

Viper

Water moccasin

Whip

BIRDS

FLIGHTLESS

Cassowary
Cormorant
Emu
Flightless cormorant
Grebe
Kakapo
Kiwi
Ostrich
Penguin
Rail
Rhea
Steamer duck
Takahe
Teal
Weka

PREDATOR

Buzzard
Eagle
Falcon
Fish-eagle
Goshawk
Harrier
Hawk
Kestrel
Kite
Merlin
Osprey
Owl
Sea-eagle
Secretarybird
Snake-eagle
Sparrowhawk
Vulture

SEA

Albatross
Auklet
Booby
Cormorant
Crane
Dovekie
Frigatebird
Fulmar
Guillemot
Gull

Jaeger
Kittiwake
Murrelet
Noddie
Northern gannet
Pelican
Petrel

Puffin
Razorbill
Shearwater
Skimmer
Skua
Tern

SONG

Cardinal
Catbird
Chickadee
Cowbird
Finch
Flycatcher
Gnatcatcher
Grosbeaks
Honeycreeper
Kingbird
Kinglet
Lark
Longspur
Magpie
Meadowlark
Mockingbird
Nightingale
Nutcracker
Nuthatch
Oriole

Parrotbills
Phoebe
Pipit
Redpoll
Robin
Scrub Jay
Scrub-birds
Shrike
Songbird
Sparrow
Starling
Swallow
Tanager
Thrush
Titmouse
Vireo
Warbler
Waxbill
Waxwing
Wren

OTHER BIRDS

Avocet

Blue Jay

Bluebird

Chickadee

Cowbird

Crow

Cuckoo

Flamingo

Flycatcher

Goose

Grouse

Hummingbird

Kingfisher

Magpie

Mockingbird

Owl

Pipit

Quail

Woodcock

Woodpecker

FISH AND CRUSTACEANS

SALTWATER

Angelfish
Anglerfish
Anthias
Barracuda
Basslets
Batfish
Blenny
Butterfly
Cardinal
Clownfish
Damsel
Dottyback
Eel
Frogfish
Goatfish
Goby
Hairtail
Hamlet
Hawkfish

Hogfish
Lionfish
Pinfish
Porgy
Puffer
Rabbitfish
Ray
Salmon
Seabream
Seahorse
Squirrelfish
Sunfish
Tang
Trigger
Viperfish
Wrasse
Grouper
Surgeonfish

FRESHWATER

American eel
Bass
Bluegill
Bullhead
Carp

Catfish
Crappie
Goldfish
Herring
Minnow

Perch pike
Pupfish
Salmon
Sturgeon

Sucker
Trout
Walleye

BRACKISH

Archer
Cichlid
Drum
Flagfish
Gar
Glass
Goby
Halfbeak

Molly
Mono
Puffer
Ray
Reedfish
Scat
Tiger

CRUSTACEANS

Barnacles
Crab
Crayfish
Hermit crab

Lobster
Prawn
Shrimp

MOLLUSCA

Abalone
Clams
Conches
Cuttlefish
Muscles
Octopus

Oysters
Scallops
Slugs
Snails
Squid

INSECTS AND OTHER ARTHROPODS

FLYING

Bee
Dragonflies
Gnat
Lightning bugs
Mayflies

Mosquito
Moth
Walking stick
Wasp

ANTS

Army
Black
Carpenter
Field
Fire

Killer
Red
Sugar
Worker

BEETLES

Billbug
Blister
Boll
Borer
Burrying
Carrion
Caterpillar hunter
Click
Dung

Firefly
Flower
Glowworm
Grapevine
Ground
Hercules
Hermit
June
Ladybug

Leaf
Longhorn
Mealy
Netwinged
Rhinoceros
Sap
Scarab

Scavenger
Stag
Stink
Tiger
Weevil
Whirligig

BUTTERFLIES

Cabbage white
Comma
Common blue
Gatekeeper
Gossamer-winged
Large white
Meadow brown
Monarch
Moth

Painted lady
Peacock
Red admiral
Ringlet
Skippers
Small tortoiseshell
Swallowtail
Tiger swallowtail

PREDATORS

Antlion
Assassin
Dragonfly
Gnat
Praying mantis

Robber fly
Tiger beetle
Water scorpion
Whiteflies

CRAWLING

Bed bug
Cockroaches
Earwigs
Fleas

Silverfish
Sow bugs
Termites
Ticks

SPIDERS

Black house

Black widow

Brazilian wandering

Brown recluse

Brown widow

Cellar

Common house

Corinnidae

Daddy long legs

Funnel-web

Garden orb weaving

Grass

Hobo

Huntsman

Jumping

Mouse

Prowling

Redback

Tarantula

Trapdoor

Wolf

Yellow sac

OTHER

Caterpillars

Centipedes

Earthworms

Horseshoe crabs

Millipedes

Mites

Scorpions

Sea spiders

Vinegarroon

SPORTS

Sports is a genre on its own and can encompass a multitude of stories and scenarios. The genre can focus on the character and/or the plot: a softball player having a chance to get to the major league, but he might lose that opportunity because of fear of success and childhood issues. Or the runner who, due to age or health, has one last chance to win the New York City Marathon.

When it comes to sports, there's football, soccer, hockey, and basketball, but there's also so much more. From the list below, you can see other varieties of sports available where you can expand and build dynamic scenes or story lines.

Sports can create passion on and off the field. Just think of the Super Bowl or the NFL playoffs. Get two people cheering on opposing teams and you're going to have a room full of emotion where tempers can fly.

Yes, a spectator can become embroiled while watching a game, but by writing about a player through narrative, dialogue and back story, you can create an unforgettable character with a variety of facets. A writer can showcase a character's drive, emotional needs, history, and goals. When writing about a character's drive to succeed in the sporting arena, you can throw obstacles one after another in his path, adding external and internal conflict and possibly bitter failure or that black moment before he wins it all.

By using sports, you can create varying plots in your story that are filled with action, emotion, and page-turning suspense. With sports, you already have an audience interested in the genre and a possible fan of the sport you are writing.

From the list below, you can decide on a specific sport or have that sport direct you down a different path. There are coaches, athletic trainers, sports and fitness nutritionists, reporters, newscasters, spouses and family members of players, and owners of sports restaurants and bars. The possibilities are almost endless. Also, don't just focus on the tried and true. Try to mix it up. What about something a little paranormal and out of this world? And remember, the sports genre can have a comedic bent to it.

PRO TEAMS

FOOTBALL NFL

Arizona Cardinals
Atlanta Falcons
Baltimore Ravens
Buffalo Bills
Carolina Panthers
Chicago Bears
Cincinnati Bengals
Cleveland Browns
Dallas Cowboys
Denver Broncos
Detroit Lions
Green Bay Packers
Houston Texans
Indianapolis Colts
Jacksonville Jaguars
Kansas City Chiefs
Las Vegas Raiders
Los Angeles Chargers

Los Angeles Rams
Miami Dolphins
Minnesota Vikings
New England Patriots
New Orleans Saints
New York Giants
New York Jets
Oakland Raiders
Philadelphia Eagles
Pittsburgh Steelers
San Francisco 49ers
Seattle Seahawks
Tampa Bay Buccaneers
Tennessee Titans
Washington Football Team * Pending
name change

BASEBALL MLB

Arizona Diamondbacks
Atlanta Braves
Baltimore Orioles
Boston Red Sox
Chicago Cubs

Chicago White Sox
Cinninnati Reds
Cleveland Indians
Colorado Rockies
Detroit Tigers

Houston Astros
Kansas City Royals
Los Angeles Angels
Los Angeles Dodgers
Miami Marlins
Milwaukee Brewers
Minnesota Twins
New York Mets
New York Yankees
Oakland Athletics

Philadelphia Phillies
Pittsburgh Pirates
San Diego Padres
San Francisco Giants
Seattle Mariners
St. Louis Cardinals
Tampa Bay Rays
Texas Rangers
Toronto Blue Jays
Washington Nationals

BASKETBALL NBA

Atlanta Hawks
Boston Celtics
Brooklyn Nets
Charlotte Hornets
Chicago Bulls
Cleveland Cavaliers
Dallas Mavericks
Denver Nuggets
Detroit Pistons
Golden State Warriors
Houston Rockets
Indiana Pacer
Indianapolis Olympians
L.A. Clippers
Los Angeles Lakers

Memphis Grizzlies
Miami Heat
Milwaukee Bucks
Minnesota Timberwolves
New Orleans Pelicans
New York Knicks
Oklahoma City Thunder
Orlando Magic
Philadelphia 76ers
Phoenix Suns
Portland Trail Blazers
Sacramento Kings
San Antonio Spurs
Toronto Raptors

HOCKEY NHL

Anaheim Ducks
Arizona Coyotes
Boston Bruins

Buffalo Sabres
Calgary Flames
Carolina Hurricanes

Chicago Blackhawks
Colorado Avalanche
Columbus Blue Jackets
Dallas Stars
Detroit Red Wings
Edmonton Oilers
Florida Panthers
Los Angeles Kings
Minnesota Wild
Montreal Canadiens
Nashville Predators
New Jersey Devils
New York Islanders

New York Rangers
Ottawa Senators
Philadelphia Flyers
Pittsburgh Penguins
San Jose Sharks
St. Louis Blues
Tampa Bay Lightning
Toronto Maple Leafs
Vancouver Canucks
Vegas Golden Knights
Washington Capitals
Winnipeg Jets

FIFA WORLD SOCCER/FOOTBALL

Austria
Azerbaijan
Bahamas
Bahrain
Bangladesh
Barbados
Belarus
Belgium
Belize
Benin
Bermuda
Bhutan
Bolivia
Bosnia and Herzegovina
Botswana
Brazil
British Virgin Islands
Brunei Darussalam

Bulgaria
Burkina Faso
Burundi
Cambodia
Cameroon
Canada
Cape Verde Islands
Cayman Islands
Central African Republic
Chad
Chile
China PR
Chinese Taipei
Columbia
Comoros
Congo
Congo DR
Costa Rica

Côte d'Ivoire
Croatia
Cuba
Curacao
Cyprus
Czech Republic
Denmark
Djibouti
Dominica
Dominican Republic
Ecuador
Egypt
El Salvador
England
Equatorial Guinea
Eritrea
Estonia
Eswatini
Ethiopia
Faroe Islands
Fiji
Finland
France
Gabon
Gambia
Georgia
Germany
Ghana
Gibraltar
Greece
Grenada
Guam
Guatemala
Guinea

Guinea-Bissau
Guyana
Haiti
Honduras
Hong Kong
Hungary
Iceland
India
Indonesia
IR Iran
Iraq
Israel
Italy
Jamaica
Japan
Jordan
Kazakhstan
Kenya
Korea DPR
Korea Republic
Kosovo
Kuwait
Kyrgyz Republic
Laos
Latvia
Lebanon
Lesotho
Liberia
Libya
Liechtenstein
Lithuania
Luxembourg
Macau
Madagascar

Malawi	Poland
Malaysia	Portugal
Maldives	Puerto Rico
Mali	Qatar
Malta	Republic of Ireland
Mauritania	Romania
Mauritius	Russia
Mexico	Rwanda
Moldova	Samoa
Mongolia	San Marino
Montenegro	Sao Tome e Principe
Montserrat	Saudi Arabia
Morocco	Scotland
Mozambique	Senegal
Myanmar	Serbia
Namibia	Seychelles
Nepal	Sierra Leone
Netherlands	Singapore
New Caledonia	Slovakia
New Zealand	Slovenia
Nicaragua	Solomon Islands
Niger	Somalia
Nigeria	South Africa
North Macedonia	South Sudan
Northern Ireland	Spain
Norway	Sri Lanka
Oman	St. Kitts and Nevis
Pakistan	St. Lucia
Palestine	St. Vincent and the Grenadines
Panama	Sudan
Papua New Guinea	Suriname
Paraguay	Sweden
Peru	Switzerland
Philippines	Syria

Tahiti

Tajikistan

Tanzania

Thailand

Timor-Leste

Togo

Tonga

Trinidad and Tobago

Tunisia

Turkey

Turkmenistan

Turks and Caicos Islands

Uganda

Ukraine

United Arab Emirates

Uruguay

US Virgin Islands

USA

Uzbekistan

Vanuatu

Venezuela

Vietnam

Wales

Yemen

Zambia

Zimbabwe

OLYMPICS

SUMMER SPORTS EVENTS

Archery
Artistic swimming
Athletics
Badminton
Baseball—softball
Basketball
Beach volleyball
Boxing
Canoe slalom
Canoe sprint
Cycling BMX
Cycling mountain bike
Cycling road
Cycling track
Diving
Equestrian dressage
Equestrian eventing
Equestrian jumping
Fencing
Football
Golf
Gymnastics artistic
Gymnastics rhythmic
Handball

Hockey
Judo
Karate
Marathon swimming
Modern pentathlon
Rowing
Rugby
Sailing
Shooting
Skateboarding
Sport climbing
Surfing
Swimming
Table tennis
Taekwondo
Tennis
Trampoline
Triathlon
Volleyball
Water polo
Weightlifting
Wrestling freestyle
Wrestling Greco-Roman

WINTER SPORTS EVENTS

Alpine skiing
Biathlon
Bobsleigh
Cross-country skiing
Curling
Figure skating
Freestyle skiing
Ice hockey

Luge
Nordic combined
Short track
Skeleton
Ski jumping
Snowboard
Speed skating

DEATH AND WEAPONS

Now we're in the fun section for suspense/thriller and mystery writers: death and weapons.

Your scene might call for weapons, whether firearms or combat (blunt, sharp, pole, ranged, or projectile), or even poison. We have listed many weapons for you to choose from, plus poisons. You could find that certain something which perfectly fits your character, whether hero, villain, or both.

Don't forget foreshadowing. For example, if a protagonist uses a gun for self-defense in your story, it should be foreshadowed earlier in the book. We should see the gun on your character's person, or perhaps somewhere in the room it's used in, before the scene is played out. If it's in your heroine's purse, show her pushing it aside as she digs through her bag to find a tissue in another scene. We might see a set of swords on the wall at a mansion as part of the story, then later one of those swords is used for self-defense or murder. Be unusual and research a weapon of your choosing and its history. Part of that history will come out in the scene. Be sure and research ways the weapon you choose can be used.

How to die? *WSW* gives you 200 different ways to die. Rather than getting shot, you might die by a manta ray sting or in a sinkhole. You'll want to dig deep and show how the character dies, and in what way another character reacts to the death. This includes the grieving process if it's someone who was close to the individual who died. Was the death slow and painful? Or fast, and the character never saw it coming? Pick when and where a death occurs and consider being unique.

Peruse this section and see what you come up with. We give you ideas. The research is up to you.

FIREARMS

TYPES OF HANDGUNS

Automatic pistols

Derringer

Multi-barreled pistols

Revolvers

Semi-automatic pistols

Single-shot pistols

POPULAR HANDGUNS WRITERS USE

Beretta

Browning

Colt

Glock

Rugar

Sig Sauer

Smith & Wesson

Walther

TYPES OF RIFLES

Bolt-action

Lever-action

Semi-automatic

Automatic

GUN MANUFACTURERS

American Longrifle

Barrett Firearms

Benelli USA

Beretta

Browning Arms Co.

Colt Defense

FN Herstal

Glock Inc.

Heckler & Koch

Henry Repeating Arms Co.

Marlin Firearms

O.F. Mossberg & Sons

Remington Outdoor

Sako Ltd.

Savage Arms

SIG Sauer Inc.

Smith & Wesson

Springfield Armory Inc.

Sturm, Rugar & Co.
Taurus International

Weatherby Inc.
Winchester Repeating Arms Co.

COMBAT WEAPONS

BLUNT

Bat
Baton
Billy-club
Brass knuckles
Cane
Chain
Club

Hammer
Nunchucks
Pipe
Shaft
Stick
Tonfa
Weighted-knuckle glove

SHARP

Axe
Battle axe
Bayonet
Blade
Chainsaw
Dagger
Dao
Dirk
Double-edged sword
Flail
Guillotine
Katana
Khopsesh
Knife
Kukri

Mace
Qama
Sabre
Scimitar
Scythe
Serrated
Stiletto
Switchblade
Sword
Sickle
Tomahawk
Urumi
War scythe
Wind and fire wheels
Yatagan

POLE WEAPONS

Barch
Gichang
Glaive
Halberd
Horseman's pick
Jangchang
Jedwart stave
Ji
Lance
Monk's spade
Naboot

Pike
Pole
Polearms
Quarterstaff
Sibat
Spear
Staff
Three-section staff
Two-section staff
War hammer
Yari

RANGED

Atlatl
Ballista
Blowgun and dart
Bolas
Boomerang
Bow and arrow
Chakrams
Compound bow
Crossbow
Dart
Harpoon
Javelin

Longbow
Rungu
Shuriken
Sling
Slingshot
Spear
Swiss arrow
Throwing axe
Throwing knife
Throwing stick
Tomahawk
Trebuchet

PROJECTILE

Airgun
Cannon
Catapult

Firearm
Grenade
Grenade launcher

Handgun

Rifle

Missile launchers

Rocket launcher

Missiles

Rockets

Musket

Shooting

Pistol

Shotgun

DEATHS

DEATHS BY ASSASSINATION

Arson/Fire
Bomb
Brass knuckles
Break neck
Car bomb
Concussive wave
Dart
Debris
Derringer
Dip in arsenic
Electrocute
Fall
Fry brain
Gauntlet
Hands/fingers/feet
Heart attack
Mortal wound

Needle
Pistol
Poison
Firing umbrella
Radiation poisoning
Revolver
Rifle
Seizure
Sniper
Sonic
Stroke
Submachine
Suffocation
Sword
Toaster/small appliances
Trained animal

ACCIDENTAL DEATHS

Acid
Airplane debris from sky
Alcohol poisoning
Auto/tanker/EMS
Bad/spoiled food
Bladed edge

Blunt force trauma
Break neck
Bridge
Broken glass
Bus
Canyon

Carbon monoxide
Catwalk fall
Choking
Cliff
Collateral damage
Concussion
Crane/heavy equipment
Dismemberment
Diving
Drowning
Drug overdose
Electrocution
Explosion
Fall
Falling items
Fire
Fly ball
Freezing to death
Frostbite
Grain bin/silo suffocation
Hand tools
Hang gliding
Helicopter
Horseback riding

Hunting
Hypothermia
Impalement
Knife
Mineshaft
Monorail
Motorcycle crash
Obstacle avoidance
Parachute
Plane
Propane tank explosion
Radiation poisoning
Saw
Shot
Slipping
Smoke inhalation
Spark
Subway
Suffocation
Sunstroke
Toxic plant
Tractor
Trapped
Tripping

DEATH BY ANIMAL/INSECT

Barracuda
Bear
Bird
Buffalo
Bull
Cow
Coyote

Crocodile/alligator
Dog
Dolphin
Eel
Elephant
Frog
Gila monster

Goring
Hippopotamus
Horse
Jellyfish
Killer whale
Lion/big cat
Manta ray
Rabid animal
Rhinoceros

Sea urchin
Shark
Snake/bite, constrictor
Spider
Stampede
Stingray
Whale
Wild boar/javelina
Wolf

MEDICAL DEATHS

Abortion
Alcohol use disorders
Allergenic reaction
Alzheimer's disease
Asthma
Cancer
Childbirth
Dementia
Disease
Drug use/overdose
Epilepsy
Heart attack
Hepatitis B
HIV/AIDS
Infection
Influenza
Iron deficiency anemia
Leukemia

Malaria
Malnutrition
Measles
Meningitis
Parasite
Parkinson's disease
Peptic ulcer disease
Pharmaceutical
Plague
Pneumonia
Pregnancy
Pulmonary
Respiratory
Salmonella
Septic
Sexually transmitted diseases
Staff infection
Tetanus

NATURAL DISASTER

Avalanche

Blizzard

Dust storm/haboob
Dynamo wave
Earthquake
Falling rock
Flash flood
Flooding
Forest fire
Hailstorm
Hurricane/typhoon
Lightning strike
Meteorite

Mudslide
Pyroclastic flow
Quicksand
Rockslide
Sinkhole
Storm surge
Tornado
Toxic gas/methane
Volcano eruption/lava flow
Wind-born debris

DEATH BY POISON

Arsenic
Baneberry
Belladonna (nightshade)
Botulinum Toxin
Carbon monoxide
Cyanide
Dandelion
Ethylene glycol (antifreeze)
False hellebore
Foxglove
Hemlock
Henbane

Lead
Mandrake
Mercury
Methanol
Monkshood
Oleander
Opium poppy
Ricin
Strychnine
Synthetic marijuana
Tabun
Wormwood

OTHER EVENT

Dehydration
Starvation

Suicide
Terrorist

LANDMARK OCCASIONS

Can't remember what holiday is where? Or what birthstone is in what month? We have a list for you! Thinking of a particular flower and wondering if it is tied to a birth month? There is a list available for birth flowers too. *WSW* also has a comprehensive list of appropriate gifts for friends or family member's landmark anniversary.

Have you always wanted to go a little deeper into the zodiac? Not just your character's sign? Along with the 12 astrology signs, we've compiled a list of the 12 astrological houses and their meanings. Sagittarius isn't just a person's sign, but it also represents the 2nd of twelve houses and covers philosophy, morals and more. If you want to delve into astrology, you can go deep with natal charts and transits or decide on a quick generalization of that person's likely astrological traits. It's all up to you.

ZODIAC SIGNS

Aquarius	January 20—February 18
Pisces	February 19—March 20
Aries	March 21—April 19
Taurus	April 20—May 20
Gemini	May 21—June 20
Cancer	June 21—July 22
Leo	July 23—August 22
Virgo	August 23—September 22
Libra	September 23—October 22
Scorpio	October 23—November 21
Sagittarius	November 22—December 21
Capricorn	December 22—January 19

ASTROLOGY HOUSES

1st ~ Ruled by Aries. Referred as a person's rising sign and ascendant. Includes self and appearance, identity, fresh starts and beginnings

2nd ~ Ruled by Taurus. Also the house of values and possessions. About material and physical environment; includes income, money and self-esteem

3rd ~ Ruled by Gemini. Consists of all communications—talking, thinking, communication devices, including phones, faxes, Internet. The 3rd house also covers siblings, neighborhoods, schools, teachers, local travel, libraries

4th ~ Ruled by Cancer. Focus is on family. Covers home, security, parents, children and a person's foundation, heredity, and the father

5th ~ Ruled by Leo. House of creativity. Ruled by romance, sex, conception, children. Includes all self-expression, creativity, drama, romance, fun and play

6th ~ Ruled by Virgo. Covers health and service, including fitness, diet and exercise, helpfulness.

7th ~ Ruled by Libra. The house includes important relationships, both personal and business. Covers contracts, marriage, and business relationships.

8th ~ Ruled by Scorpio. Focus is on intimacy, includes death, sex, transformation, secrets and mysteries. Also covers other people's money and property.

9th ~ Ruled by Sagittarius. Covers religion, philosophy, morals and ethics. Also includes, risk, higher education, and gambling.

10th ~ Ruled by Capricorn. The house of career. Public part of a person's astrological chart. This house includes honors, fame, discipline, fathers, and fatherhood.

11th ~ Ruled by Aquarius. This house is ruled by friendship, community and acquaintances. The 11th house also focuses on destiny, hopes and dreams, and the power of the collective.

12th ~ Ruled by Pisces. The house of the subconscious. This house includes jails, asylums, hospitals, and institutions. It is also the house of Karma and Secrets.

BIRTH STONES

January	Garnet
February	Amethyst
March	Aquamarine
April	Diamond
May	Emerald
June	Pearl or Alexandrite
July	Ruby
August	Peridot
September	Sapphire
October	Opal or Tourmaline
November	Topaz or Citrine
December	Zircon, Blue Topaz, or Turquoise

BIRTH FLOWERS

January	Carnation and snowdrop
February	Violet and primrose
March	Daffodil and jonquil
April	Daisy and sweet pea
May	Lily of the valley and hawthorn
June	Rose and honeysuckle
July	Larkspur and water lily
August	Gladiolus and poppy
September	Aster and morning glory
October	Marigold and cosmos
November	Chrysanthemum
December	Narcissus and holly

ANNIVERSARIES

Anniversary year	Anniversary gifts	Anniversary flower
1st	Paper	Carnation
2nd	Cotton	Lily of the valley
3rd	Leather	Sunflower, fuchsia
4th	Fruit, flowers	Geranium, hydrangea
5th	Wood	Daisy
6th	Iron, candy	Calla lily
7th	Wool, copper	Freesia
8th	Bronze	Lilac
9th	Willow, pottery	Bird of paradise
10th	Tin, aluminum	Daffodil
11th	Steel	Tulips
12th	Silk, linen	Peony
13th	Lace	Chrysanthemum
14th	Ivory (banned), gold jewelry	Orchid, dahlia
15th	Crystal	Rose
20th	China	Aster, day lily
25th	Silver	Iris
30th	Pearl	Lily of the valley, sweet pea
35th	Coral	Poppy
40th	Ruby	Gladiolas, nasturtium
45th	Sapphire	Blue iris, delphinium
50th	Gold	Yellow roses, violets

U. S. HOLIDAYS

New Year's Day	January 1
Civil Rights Day	January (3rd Monday)
Groundhog Day	February 2
Valentine's Day	February 14
President's Day	February (3rd Monday)
St. Patrick's Day	March 17
Easter	March or April (varies)
April Fools' Day	April 1
Mother's Day	May (2nd Sunday)
Memorial Day	May (Last Monday)
Father's Day	June (3rd Sunday)
Independence Day	July 4
Labor Day	September (1st Monday)
Indigenous Peoples' Day	October (2nd Monday)
Halloween	October 31
Veterans Day	November 11
Thanksgiving	November (4th Thursday)
Christmas Eve	December 24
Christmas	December 25
New Year's Eve	December 31

COLORS

Colors are fun. Blue doesn't just have to be boring blue. It can be misty, royal, sky, or smoke blue. What about baby or electric blue? *WSW* has over 250 various colors to choose from.

Don't discount the importance of color in writing. Color can dramatically create a vivid scene. Imagine a character walking into the kitchen, getting a glass of milk from the refrigerator, and setting it on the counter. Next, layer the scene with color. Add mint green to the walls, chrome to the fridge, and charcoal to the counters and floor. By adding color to the kitchen, depth is also added to a scene or story.

Color not only creates visual depth to a scene but can also create mood and emotion. When a person reads or sees a particular color, she or he usually has a preconceived idea of what that color means, which can conjure a specific emotion or memory in their mind. Red often relates to passion, love, or war, while yellow instills thoughts of friendship, happiness, or springtime.

Creating color can add contrasts, too. Imagine a room of muted colors and your character is dressed in bright red or vice versa. Color can also reveal a person's character. What about someone who's timid or unassuming, but her house or apartment is filled with vibrant colors? Or a person who always dresses in yellow because he wants to be seen or noticed at all times?

Color, though, can be tricky. Remember your character when adding color to your scenes. A truck driver is usually not going to look at a mound of dirt and see the various shades of brown. Also, a chef is going to be highly in tune with color when it comes to photographed images of his food in national magazines or blogs.

BLACK

Black: white is the opposite
Blue-black: similar to the sun against a raven with a hint of blue
Coal: black
Ebony: black
Humus: hint of brown with black, very dark brown
Inky-black: has a depth or gleam to black
Jet: a flat black, the color of the mineraloid jet
Licorice: a light black, the color of the black candy
Lignite: brown-black coal
Metal: black sheen with gray
Midnight: black or darker shade of color
Obsidian: black
Onyx: the color of the gemstone
Pitch: flat black
Raven: black
Tar: black

BLUE

Azure: color of clear blue sky
Baby blue: light blue, pastel blue
Celestial blue: sky blue
Cobalt: deep blue pigment containing cobalt and aluminum oxides.
Dove gray: grayish-blue or brown
Electric blue: deep glowing blue
Gentian: deep rich blue with hint of purple
Glaucous: blue-gray or blue-green, coating on grapes or plums
Hyacinth: deep purplish-blue
Indigo: color between blue and purple
Juniper: gray or green-blue
Lapis lazuli: deep blue
Misty blue: very light blue

Periwinkle: light blue with hint of purple
Powder blue: very light blue
Prussian blue: dark blue
Royal blue: deep blue/purple
Sapphire: saturated blue
Sky blue: clear blue sky
Smoke: blue/gray

BROWN

Auburn: reddish-brown or dark ginger
Biscuit: light tan
Bronze: metallic brown that matches the alloy
Brown
Caramel: lighter brown, color of the candy
Chestnut: medium reddish shade of brown
Chocolate: dark brown that looks like chocolate
Cinnamon: brownish-red, hint of orange
Cocoa: light brown
Dove gray: grayish-blue or brown
Dun: light brown, may have hint of gray
Dusty road: light brown
Ginger: reddish-brown, lighter brown with hint of orange
Golden: lighter brown with hint of yellow
Hay: light brown or tan; May have hint of yellow
Hazel: light yellowish-brown with a hint of green
Honey: golden brown
Humus: black or dark brown
Kelp: greenish-brown
Leather: brown, medium in color
Mahogany: reddish dark brown
Molasses: dark brown
Teakwood: ranges from yellowish-white to golden brown

GRAY

Ash: light gray, can add to other color for combinations
Charcoal: dark gray
Dove gray: medium gray with a slight tint of pink or blue
Dun: light gray with brown
Harbor gray: multi-toned gray
Pewter: between silver and deep gray and has a mild luster
Salt and pepper: mix of black and white and be light to dark
Shadow: can be dark gray or used to darken any hue
Silver: gray-white, can be metallic
Slate : bluish-gray or dark gray
Smoke: light to dark gray with white to blue hint
Smoked glass: gray to dark gray
Soot: grayish-brown
Steel: dark gray to bluish-gray
Steel: metallic light to medium gray, hint of blue
Tarnish gray: added to gray, can be considered metallic

GREEN

Aquamarine: transparent bluish-green
Cactus: light to medium green
Chartreuse: halfway between yellow and green that was named because of its resemblance to the green color of one of the French liqueurs
Emerald: bright, bold green
Grass: light to medium or bold green
Green
Jade: pale to dark green
Leaf: medium green
Moss: dark green with yellow tint
Olive: light to medium green, somewhat dull in color
Smaragdine: see emerald green
Teal: bold medium to dark bluish-green

Terre verte: neutral cool green
Viridescent: from yellow, chartreuse, whitish-green; then darken to green.
Xanadu: gray green, color of philodendron leaf

LIGHT COLORS

Alabaster: light yellowish-pink to grayish-pink
Ash: very light gray that can be added to other colors
Beige: pale tan, off-white
Bleached: added to color to whiten
Buff: cream, off-white, from a yellow to pink or tan hue
Chalky: added white to any color, can be very pale yellow or gray
Ecru: very pale tan
Eggshell: very pale yellow or brown
Hay: golden hue
Hazel: light yellowish-brown golden color
Marble: pale yellow or white
Peach: usually paler than the actual peach fruit
Rosy: pink mixed with red hue
Wheat: light golden tan

ORANGE

Amber: ranges are yellow-orange-brown-red
Apricot: like the fruit, light yellowish-orangish-pinkish color
Carrot hue
Copper: reddish-brown, can be metallic
Fire: bright orange, can have mix of yellow and red
Fulvous: brownish-yellow
Gold: yellowish-orange, can be metallic
Henna: orange-brown hue
Ocher: yellowish to reddish-orange
Ochre: from yellow to deep orange or brown
Orange

Pumpkin: bright to medium orange
Saffron: orange-yellow
Tangerine: bright medium orange
Tiger: bright or bold orange

PINK

Ballet slipper: pale to light pink
Blush: medium bright tone of red-violet
Bubblegum: light pink
Coral: reddish or pinkish shade of orange
Cotton candy: light to bright pink
Flamingo: light to medium pink, the color of the bird
Fuchsia: purplish-red
Guava: warm pink
Hot pink: vibrant and bold pink
Pale pink: very light pink
Peach: paler than most fruit peaches
Punch: pink with reddish undertones
Rouge: reddish-pink, from light to dark
Salmon: range of pale pinkish-orange to light pink
Taffy: light pink to pink with brown undertones
Watermelon: medium pink

PURPLE

Amethyst: vibrant purple, violet
Deep purple: dark purple
Grape: dark purple, may have hint of red
Indigo: between blue and violet
Iris: shades ranging from blue-violet to violet
Lavender: light tone of violet
Lilac: pale to dark violet tone
Magenta: purplish-red, reddish-purple, or a mauvish-crimson color

Mauve: pale bluish-purple

Orchid: bright rich purple

Periwinkle: lavender blue or mix of blue and violet

Plum: purple with a brownish-gray undertone

Puce: dark red or purple-brown

Purple

Royal purple: deep vibrant purple

Violet: more bluish tones and less saturated than purple

RED

Amaranth: medium to dark red

Auburn: reddish-brown

Blood: deep red

Bronze: reddish-brown, might be metallic

Cinnabar: vibrant, bright red

Cinnamon: brownish-red

Copper: reddish-orange

Crimson: deep bold red

Falu: deep red

Fire: bright red with orange

Garnet: dark red with brown hues

Hazel: reddish-brown and can have green or gray flecks

Lobster red: bright red

Magenta: purplish-red, reddish-purple, or a mauvish-crimson color

Mahogany: reddish-dark brown

Maroon: dark, dull reddish-brown

Red

Rose: bright red, color of red rose

Rosy: pinkish-red

Ruby: deep red, color of gemstone

Ruddy: healthy red, description of person's face

Rufous: reddish-brown or brownish-red

Rust: reddish-brown, might have orange tint

Sanguine: reddish-brown, color of dried blood
Scarlet: bright, vibrant red
Sepia: reddish-brown
Strawberry: bright red
Tarnish: applied to a color, usually metal
Vermillion: brilliant, bright red
Wine: dark red, red wine hue

WHITE

Alabaster: translucent with a white tone
Bleach blond: white with silver or golden hue
Bone: between white and yellow, very light shade of white
Chalky: off-white with yellow or gray tones
Cream: hint of yellow
Eburnean: slightly yellow shade, close to ivory
Eggshell: more white than pale brown
Ivory: white with a hint of yellow
Marble: usually streaked with gray or other colors, usually not one color
Milky: white, thick
Salt: white
White

YELLOW

Amber: yellowish-orange
Banana: bright vibrant yellow
Blond: yellow, close to honey
Bumblebee: vibrant bright yellow
Canary: vibrant yellow
Corn: light to medium yellow
Dijon: earthy, dusty tan with yellow tint
Eggnog: very pale yellow
Ginger: sandy or reddish-brown

Golden: yellow with brown hues

Hawk brown: yellowish-brown, or grayish-brown

Hay: light brown or tan; may have hint of yellow

Honey: golden-brown or tan

Lemon: bright, vibrant yellow

Mikado: bold yellow

Mustard: dull dark yellow

Ochre: from yellow to deep orange or brown

Pineapple: light to medium yellow, color of the fruit

Saffron: orange-yellow

Sallow: pale yellow, sickly yellow

Sandy: light brown, varies from yellow, gray to red tints

Sienna: yellowish-brown

Straw: light to medium yellow, may have tan or brown tones

Tawny: brownish-yellow or tan with yellow

Teakwood: yellowish-brown

Wheat: resembles the light yellow of the wheat grain

Yellow

OTHER

Iridescent: lustrous rainbow-like colors, can be seen in oil slicks or bubbles

Metallic: resembling polished metal

Mottled: specks or dots across lighter color

Neon: depends on the gas, tubes, and other factors. Vibrant colors

Rainbow: from outer to inner rings—red, orange, yellow, green, blue, indigo, and violet

WRITER TECHNIQUES

What's in a writer's toolkit is the most important part of their career. Cheyenne and H.D. have given workshops and talks on a variety of tools over the past twenty years and have gathered ideas for your toolkit. We are all different, and we each use our tools to suit our own writing methods. Sometimes all it takes is one new idea that can make our writing processes easier and even richer. *WSW* gives you ideas that can trigger your creativity and help your writing process.

When you attend writer's workshops, conferences, and conventions, you are often bombarded with an enormous amount of information. What do you do with all that you've learned? The best way is to take a couple of ideas, the ones that call to you, and start on those. See if they fill your needs and help you in your writing and creative process. Not all of them will, but you'll find something that does. Sometimes it's the little things that make a difference.

A decade ago, after ten years' experience, Cheyenne started to use a new way to organize her thoughts in writing and it made a huge difference in her process. You can always learn something new, so keep your mind open to possibilities.

Fill your own toolbox with ideas that work for you. Find new ways to make your process even more effective if you have difficulties in any area. Keep your mind open.

When it comes to our writer's toolkit, sometimes we have deeper questions. If you have questions on any methods we suggest, feel free to email Cheyenne and H.D. at bellamediamanagement@gmail.com and we'll be happy to help.

EDITING TECHNIQUES

CHECKLIST

Are sentences all one length or do they vary?

Are the character's actions explained by a believable motive?

Avoid all capital letters.

Avoid complicated word choices.

Avoid using the same word. Change it up with a thesaurus.

Check for correct formatting for italics and capitalization.

Check for correct punctuation.

Check for pacing.

Check for spelling mistakes.

Check for stilted dialogue and remove.

Check for syntax. Do you have words that appear out of place from the rest of your dialogue or narrative.

Check for that vs. who.

Check if a scene or chapter accomplishes what you intended.

Check if writing consistently in first person, second person, third person or third personal omniscient point of view?

Correct homonyms.

Cut overly long sentences to avoid confusion.

Cut wisely—avoid deleting emotion.

Do your action/suspense scenes have short sentences to increase tension?

Do your chapter endings have hooks or are they neatly tied up?

Do your characters have individual goals?

Does the story and each scene have a conflict?

Does the story have a black moment?

During dialogue do you use action tags instead of 'replied' or 'said', etc.?

Eliminate cliche dialogue and general cliches.

Establish point of view in a scene as soon as feasible.

Excessive telling of character's backstory or physical attributes before they show up with dialogue or action?

Has the character's emotions been told or shown?

Hyphenate modifiers when needed.

Introducing too many characters at once?

Is the villain in the story one-dimensional? Do they have any redeeming qualities?

Is there a climax and resolution to the story?

Point of view—avoid head hopping. Keep to one character per scene if possible.

Read aloud to remove clunky or awkward language.

Reduce prepositions.

Remove unnecessary adverbs and adjectives.

Remove passive words.

Show don't tell—remove areas where the narrative or dialogue informs the reader and replace with action, dialogue, thoughts, senses, and feelings.

Too much or too little narrative summary? Bouncing from scene to scene? Long passages with nothing happening?

Try to include as many senses as possible within a scene—hearing, sight, smell, taste, touch, kinesthetic, and organic.

SIMILES

Exercise is like torture to her
Grandma is as stubborn as a mule
Grandpa is as crazy as a cat on caffeine
He follows her around like a puppy
He is as interesting as an empty notebook
He treats her like a princess
He turns up like a bad penny
He's as dumb as a post
He's as happy as a puppy chewing on its favorite toy
He's as quiet as a feather drifting to the ground
He's as smart as a whip
He's as tall as a skyscraper
He's slyer than a fox
Her day had been a roller coaster of emotions
Her expression is like a blank piece of paper
Her hair is like molten gold
Her hair is straight as a board
Her head feels like a troll is pounding against her skull
Her heart pounds like a basketball in a washing machine
Her laugh is like nails scraping across a chalkboard
Her memory is like a sieve
His face is like a gargoyle
His retelling of the incident is clear as mud
His stomach feels like it's lined with concrete
It was as difficult as finding a needle in a haystack
My brother is as strong as an ox
My cousin is as quick as a cat
My dad is as brave as a lion
My sister is like a parrot the way she repeats everything

My skin crawls as if a thousand insects are skittering over it
My spine is like an iron rod encased in ice
She feels as light as a feather
She might as well be as blind as a bat the way she loses things
She sings like a screech owl
She walks like she's in a beauty pageant
She's always as busy as a bee
She's as colorful as a box of crayons
She's as free as a bird
She's as militant as a sergeant
Snow falls as soft as white cotton
That bug is as dead as a doornail
The floor is as smooth as glass
The park is as clean as a whistle now
The sisters fought like cats and dogs
They work together like a colony of ants
Watching the movie was like watching grass grow
You're as much fun as a barrel of monkeys
You're as sweet as honey

METAPHORS

Crickets are the stars singing
He is a giant
He is an open book
He is a prince
He is hell on wheels
He is king of his castle
Her boys are sweet angels
Her brain is a vault
Her emotions are a roller coaster
Her eyes are blue pools
Her girls are little devils
Her heart is ice
Her mind is a trap
Her tears were a river
He's a jackass
His brain is a computer
His nose is a hook
His stomach is lead
His voice is a bullhorn
Life is a race
Life is a wheel of fortune
Love is a game
Mom is the Energizer Bunny
My brother is a turd
My little sister is a diamond in the rough
My mom is a rock
My sister is a free spirit
She is a brilliant star
She is a chicken
She is a dictionary

She is a monster
She is a princess
She is a whirlwind
She is the queen mother
She is the warden of the neighborhood
She lives in a zoo
She was a prisoner in her marriage
She is a firecracker
She is bad news
Snowflakes are winter's kisses
That boy is a pig
That girl is a glass half-full
That girl is a songbird
That man is a rotten apple
Their faces are mirrors
The water around the island is blue glass.
They are sheep
They are snowbirds

WRITING TOOLS

CONFLICT

Without conflict there is no story. Conflict is the suspense, the means of driving the plot of your story, and it's what creates your character's individuality. Always remember, there is internal and external conflict. Internal is within your character, what makes him become the person he is. It involves two driving needs or wants where if he chooses one, he will lose the other. External conflicts are events, people, or a particular force/instrument outside of the character that creates tension and motivation. Powerful conflict involves two opposing forces that have equal strength. The higher the stakes, the stronger the conflict.

The following list is widely believed to be the seven basic conflicts in literature. Taking a look at the list might spark an idea for a new novel. All literature contains at least one of these basic conflicts. What you bring to the table is your own talent and creativity to write something that hasn't been done in that way before. The basic conflicts might be the same, but your writing should never be. You are unique and your work should reflect that.

7 BASIC CONFLICTS

Character vs. Character

Character vs. Fate

Character vs. Nature

Character vs. Self

Character vs. Society

Character vs. Supernatural

Character vs. Technology

WAYS TO BRAINSTORM

Sometimes we are just plain stuck. We've written ourselves into a corner or we aren't sure which path to take, or even where a path might exist to begin with. *WSW* shows you a variety of ways to brainstorm—if one way doesn't work for you, try another. You might use different methods at different times. Be flexible!

When you start brainstorming, remember you're the one in control. Pick an idea or phrase. Then start asking questions about it. How? Where? Why? And my favorite, "What if?" Expand on each question. Delete, delete, delete if nothing works, and start over again. You are, after all, the creator of your story.

Feel free to add music to your brainstorming session. It's only natural to add another creative technique to help you with ideas. Dark, emotional music to fit a tense scene, or light and airy notes in an uplifting chapter. Various playlists that you can select to help you are out on the net. H.D. has been known to listen to Gregorian chant music to brainstorm that dark, gut-wrenching moment in her novel. Cheyenne often listens to the soundtrack for *Pirates of the Caribbean* when writing a scene that needs energy, *Gladiator* in more dramatic situations, and so on.

Nothing beats brainstorming in a group. Grab a friend or family member if you're not in a critique group and have them help you. Through *WSW,* you already have phrases you can choose from. Snag one from the list and have people in the group expand on it. The sky's the limit. Be inventive, be crazy, and, most importantly, have fun!

BRAINSTORMING

Add a different perspective

Ask how, what, when, where, who, why, why, why

Ask, "How do we get from location 1 to location 2?"

Ask "What if…"

Big picture thinking

Brainstorm to music

Brainstorm with someone new

Brainstorm with sticky notes

Come up with X ideas for a topic

Consider who your audience is

Critique partners

Critiquing or judgment of ideas

Cubing—look at one word/item/topic from six different perspectives

Determine the purpose of the story

Doodle images

Draw pictures

Freewrite

Garden

Generate random ideas

Interrogate the main character

Journal

List a character's likes and dislikes

Magazine pictures cut out and put onto a posterboard in a collage

Meditate

Mind map

Pre-brainstorm alone, then brainstorm with peers

Pretend to be in someone else's shoes

Question subordinate characters; ask what they think of the main characters

Question what could have been done differently after reading a book

Question your characters
Randomly search an encyclopedia
Read an unfamiliar topic or subject
Read other books on the same topic or theme
Research a favorite topic
Round-robin
Storyboard with notecards
Storyboard with sticky notes
Trigger prompt—word, sentence, paragraph, quote, poetry, letter. music, images
Visit a travel blog or browse a travel magazine
Visualization
Word or object association
Workout
Write a letter
Write character histories

PANTSING & OUTLINES

Instead of pantsing (writing by the seat of your pants rather than planning ahead) or outlining, we call the process *Organizing Your Thoughts*.

Cheyenne started out as a pantser, but developed her own method, using a hybrid version. She writes out an idea for each chapter on a separate sheet of paper or a new page in a Word doc, then uses bullet points for ideas she wants to use within that chapter. Those ideas always morph and she adds in additional chapters as she goes, or changes her ideas entirely. She considers her outline—her thought organization—to be a living, breathing method that allows her the flexibility of pantsing, but that also gives her a path and a goal. Once she started using this method a decade ago, her writing flowed easier and faster.

Over the years prior to this method, she used a wide variety of ways to attempt to better organize her thoughts, while maintaining flexibility, and often struggled with the process. This method better helps her develop and flesh out her plots and keeps her focused on her ultimate goal.

H.D. chooses to do a mix of pantsing and outlining in her writing process. She also started out as a pantser, but realized over time that she needed to plot several sections of her story if she didn't want to rewrite again and again. She mainly works from scene to scene in a linear fashion unless a certain scene pops in her head that is pivotal to the plot or character.

Each scene outline is bulleted and starts with the character's goal, motivation and the scene's conflict. From there she adds to it, going deeper by adding items related to setting, the action, creating the hook at the end of the chapter or scene, and so forth. Before she gets into any great detail, though, she also creates character bios and goes over their physical traits, what secrets they might be hiding, their strengths and weaknesses, their history as to where they lived and who they lived with, and whether or not they had any childhood traumas.

It's all up to you how detailed you want to get.

PANTSING

Write by the "seat of your pants" with an idea and let it flow with no physical structure.

WE CALL IT ORGANIZING THOUGHTS, NOT OUTLINING

Hybrid outlining: write the chapter number, create an idea for the chapter in a sentence for the title, and add bullet points for things you would like included. This outline evolves—can change, be moved, added to, deleted, etc.

Sticky notes for scenes on posterboard: Write ideas on sticky notes, then organize them on a posterboard. Notes can be moved as needed.

Timeline: Draw a timeline on a piece of paper or in a document. Write in ideas along the timeline.

Traditional outlining: Write ideas in detail for each chapter.

Storyboard scenes: Use notes on index cards and organize. You can change the order as needed. Use push pins and fasten on a corkboard.

MOTIVES AND GOALS

MOTIVES

A person will die
A pet will die
Abandon one's beliefs
Accepting an offer
Accumulate wealth
Acquire money
Acquire power
Act in self-defense
Adopting a child
Avenge a death
Avoid a war
Avoid dark thoughts
Avoid death
Avoid pain
Avoid stress
Await traumatic news
Become a leader
Become a parent
Being abandoned
Being fired from work
Being punctual
Being sued
Better one's appearance
Better oneself
Breaking an animal

Breaking another human emotionally
Buy a home/material item
Change a career
Compete in a project
Conspire with another
Creating a loving home
Creating chaos
Death of a loved one
Defeat an enemy
Destroy an enemy
Escape a car accident
Escape a fear or phobia
Escape a killer
Escape an abusive relationship
Escape destiny
Escape financial ruin
Escape grief/loss
Escape homelessness
Escape loneliness
Escape the past
Explore a geographical area
Expose a secret
Face a fear
Failing a class
Fighting an illness

Fitting in
Forgiving oneself
Gain acceptance
Gain control over one's life
Gain control over others
Get a new job
Get into a relationship
Get out of a relationship
Give up a child
Hide an object from another
Host a surprise party
Inspire a loved one
Invent something new
Keep a secret
Make a new friend
Master a skill
Meet someone
Obstruct justice
Overcome a gambling habit
Overcome a physical trauma
Overcome a sexual habit
Overcome abuse
Physical pain
Power
Prove someone wrong

Provide for the family
Pursue a talent or skill
Realize a dream
Rebel against person/object
Reconcile with a family member
Recover what is lost
Relocate
Revenge against another
Rule the world
Save a marriage
Save adult
Save child
Save family
Save humanity
Settling a dispute
Shameful act
Silencing a witness
Solve a problem
Survive a natural disaster
The thrill of chasing person/dream
To become popular
To preserve moral goal
Trying to contact someone
Uncovering a mystery

PSYCHOLOGICAL/EMOTIONAL NEEDS

Acceptance
Affection
Analyze
Appreciation
Approval
Attention
Authenticity

Autonomy
Belonging
Capability
Celebration
Challenge
Choice
Clarity

Cleanliness

Closeness

Communication

Community

Companionship

Competence

Confidence

Consciousness

Consistency

Contribution

Control

Creativity

Dignity

Ease

Effectiveness

Efficacy

Empathy

Equality

Faith

Family

Forgiveness

Freedom

Fulfilled

Growth

Harmony

Healing

Helpful

Honesty

Hope

Humor

Inclusion

Independence

Inspiration

Integrity

Intimacy

Joy

Kindness

Lack of prejudice

Learning

Love

Loyalty

Morality

Mourning

Mutual respect

Order

Participation

Passion

Peace of mind

Play

Pleasure

Power

Presence

Privacy

Productive

Protection

Purpose

Rejuvenation

Respect/respect self

Responsibility

Safety

Salvation

Self-acceptance

Self-esteem

Self-expression

Sharing

Space

Spontaneity

Stability

Status	Transparency
Stimulation	Trusted
Supported	Understood
Tenderness	Valued
To be needed	Variety
Touching	Worthy

CHARACTER GOALS

FITNESS GOALS

1000 stairs challenge
Athletic team tryouts
Ballerina to perform in a production
Ballerina tryouts
Become healthy
Bicycle tour
Bodybuilding competition
Boxing competition
Cheerleading competition
Coaching job
Compete in a triathlon
Dancing competition
Diving competition
Do more yoga
Extreme sports
Fencing competition
Get fit
Get in the Olympics
Golfing competition
Gymnastics competition
Hike to top of mountain
Learn how to dance
Learn how to skate

Learn martial arts
Learn to rollerblade
Lose body mass/decrease body fat
Marathon running
Martial arts competition
Paralympic competition
Polo competition
Physical Education teacher
Race-walk competition
Rodeo competition
Rugby game
Sculpt muscles
Skating competition
Skiing competition
Spelunking
Strengthen
Surfing competition
Swimming competition
Tennis or racquetball competition
Track and field competition
Weight loss
Wheelchair racing

FINANCIAL GOALS

Affiliate marketing

AirBNB

Become a virtual assistant
Childcare
Direct sales
Drive for Uber, Lyft, Door Dash
Earn a million/billion dollars
Earn a real estate license
Earn more money
Flip houses
Food delivery
Freelance editing
Get a renter
Get a roommate
Get paid to complete surveys
Go antiquing and resell items
Go back to school to get a degree
Grocery delivery
Handyman work
Have a yard/garage sale
Home party plan
Improve credit
Make a budget

Make money on YouTube
Mow lawns
Offer skills on Fiverr or Upwork
Online teaching
Open an eBay or Etsy store
Pay off bills/debt free
Pet sitting
Plow driveways
Publish an eBook
Recycle cans or scrap metal
Reduce bills
Renovate home to resell
Rent homes
Save money
Sell handmade items
Social media manager for businesses
Start a bed and breakfast
Start a blog and have advertisements
Start a business
Start a stock portfolio
Tutor

PROFESSIONAL/BUSINESS/EMPLOYMENT GOALS

Attract top-notch employees
Better customer retention
Better customer service
Better employee retention
Boost employee morale
Buy a franchise
Buy/sell properties
Climb the corporate ladder
Create a mission statement
Create better website

Cultivate new clients
Cut costs
Develop a social media presence
Develop new products
Develop sales pitch
Enhance existing products
Establish online chat assistance
Find new business idea
Further education
Get a new job

Increase production
Increase revenue
Job with benefits
Launch new products
Make better work decisions
Make more cold calls
Make more sales
More people under you in sales
Operate more efficiently
Set up and track goals
Set up employee benefit plan
Start a brick and mortar business
Start an online business
Survey customers
Work toward a dream job
Working from home

ADVENTURE GOALS

Backpack Europe
Big game photography in Africa
Bungee jumping in New Zealand
Camp in the Smoky Mountains
Coffee and a pastry in a Paris cafe
Drink in a pub in Germany
Eat a cannoli in Italy
Explore a cave in Bermuda
Go on a foodie tour in Hong Kong
Go to a pagoda in Japan
Go to a Scottish castle
Go to a temple in Beijing
Go to the French Riviera
Go up in a hot air balloon in Turkey
Have a beer in Ireland
Have bangers and mash in London
Have coffee in Vietnam
Hike a mountain in Tanzania
Hike in the Sonoran Desert
Hike the Grand Canyon
Hike through Europe
Parasailing in Cape Town
Ride a camel in Egypt
Ride a gondola in Venice
Ride an elephant in Thailand
Scuba dive in the Galapagos
Search for treasure
See a psychic in Sedona
See the aurora borealis
Skydive in Dubai
Surfing in Australia
Take a cruise to Bora Bora
Travel around the world
Visit a glacier in Antarctica
Visit an archaeological dig
Visit an Italian glass-making factory
Visit every continent
Visit every state in the U.S.
Visit Monaco
Visit Stonehenge
Visit the Giza Pyramids
Whitewater rafting in Costa Rica

OTHER GOALS

Astronomy—find a new star
Be kinder
Become a mentor
Become physically active
Become popular
Catch up on rest
Date nights
Don't worry about small matters
Escape society
Express gratitude
Floss regularly
Fly a kite
Gain acceptance
Get more sleep
Get on or off of social media
Go for walks
Have a baby
Learn a foreign language
Learn how to paint with pastels

Learn public speaking
Learn to say "no"
Make new friends
Meet neighbors
Modeling competition
Plan a dinner party
Plan a girl's night
Plan a playdate for kids
Read for pleasure
Relax more
Set measurable goals
Spend more time with the kids
Start a hobby
Start a journal
Start exercising
Stop biting nails
Take care of health
Take classes
Volunteer

GENRES/SUBGENRES

When you select a genre, if you don't know much on the subject, do your research. You can't have a whodunit without a killer. Well, you might, but we can bet your reader is going to be disappointed.

Knowing your genre is important. Each has a purpose and unique features. By selecting a certain genre, you've also created a promise to your readers. You can't write crime fiction when you are missing a number of factors: a criminal, a crime, an investigation. Genres can be blurred or step slightly out of the traditional genre and even cross over to other genres. At the same time, your reader has basic assumptions, and by not giving your audience certain key elements of a genre, you've broken an unspoken promise.

Yes, there are limits to a genre, but rules can be broken too. Be creative, think outside of the formula, but keep to the genre structure. Otherwise, your story might fall flat, and feel contrived or boring.

Expectations are important. They run through everyone's lives. When a consumer enters a craft store, she has a preconceived idea of what products will be offered. If she sees only items from a hardware store, she is not only going to be confused, she may become angry and quickly leave the store. Same with your reader—if she starts reading what she expects to be a romance and finds no growing relationship and conflict between two of the main characters, but instead only murder and mayhem, she will quickly power off her e-reader. She might be upset to the point she will leave a bad review or warn other readers about your book.

Maybe you don't know where your book fits in, or what genre you want to write. *WSW* includes basic genres and subgenres for you to go through for more ideas to spark your imagination.

Choosing a genre on Amazon and other distribution sites is very important. The more specific the genre, the more likely a reader will discover your book. There are thousands and thousands of books under mystery, but if you drill down to a more specific genre like cozy culinary mystery, the ability to be found on a bestseller list can dramatically increase. Also, if you manage to get your book on a smaller bestseller list, your book is less likely to drop off that list as quickly.

Adding the right keyword can also increase your odds of being discoverable. The following lists in *Writer's Secret Weapon* can help you find that particular keyword or genre you might have missed otherwise.

GENERAL GENRES AND KEYWORDS

FICTION

Action and adventure
Alternate history
Anthology
Chick lit
Children's literature
Comic book
Coming-of-age
Crime
Drama
Erotica
Fairytale
Fantasy
Graphic novel
Historical fiction
Horror

Mystery
Paranormal romance
Picture book
Poetry
Political thriller
Romance
Romantic Suspense
Satire
Science fiction
Short story
Suspense
Thriller
Urban Fantasy
Young adult

NON-FICTION

Art
Autobiography
Biography
Book review
Business
Cookbook
Diary
Dictionary
Encyclopedia

Guide
Health
History
Journal
Math
Memoir
Money
Non-fiction
Prayer

Religion, spirituality, and new age Self help
Review Textbook
Science Travel

SUBGENRES AND KEYWORDS

BIOGRAPHIES & MEMOIRS

Arts & Literature—Entertainers
Arts & Literature—Composers & Musicians
Biographies & Memoirs
Arts & Literature—Movie Directors
Historical—Africa
Historical—Asia
Historical—Canada
Historical—Europe
Historical—Latin America
Historical—Middle East
Historical—Military & Wars—American Civil War
Historical—Military & Wars—American Revolution
Historical—Military & Wars—Branches
Historical—Military & Wars—Cold War
Historical—Military & Wars—Vietnam War
Historical—Military & Wars—World War I
Historical—Military & Wars—World War II
Leaders & Notable People—Presidents & Heads of State
Leaders & Notable People—Religious
Sports & Outdoor

BUSINESS AND MONEY

Biographies & Primers—Inspiration
Business Life
Economics—Unemployment

Education & Reference—MBA
Entrepreneurship & Small Business—Legal Guides
Entrepreneurship & Small Business—Startups
Industries
Investing—Investing Basics
Job Hunting & Careers—Interviewing
Management & Leadership—Teams
Personal Finance—Financial Planning
Technology

CHILDREN'S BOOKS

Baby-2
Ages 3-5
Ages 6-8
Ages 9-12
Fantasy & Magic—Coming of Age
Fantasy & Magic—Sword & Sorcery
Mystery & Thrillers—Detectives
Mystery & Thrillers—Fantasy & Supernatural
Mystery & Thrillers—Spies
Science Fiction—Action & Adventure
Science Fiction—Aliens
Science Fiction—Time Travel

COMIC AND GRAPHICS

Action-packed
Animals
Art Books
Bandes Dessinées
Collections
Comics—Publication by era
Dark

Disturbing
Everyday Life
Female Protagonists
Fun
Gods & Goddesses
Gory
Graphic Novels

Historical & Literary—Biography
Humorous
Manga
Martial Arts
Military
Mystery, Thriller & Suspense
Omnibus
Politicians
Pulp
Racy
Robots & Androids
Romantic
Samplers

Scary
Seasonal
Single Issues
Spies
Sports
Steampunk
Vampires
Vengeful
Web Comics
Werewolves & Shifters
Western
Witches & Wizards
Zombies

EROTICS

Action & Adventure
Adult Fairy Tales
Alpha Males
Angels
BBW
BDSM
Billionaires
Cowboys
Devils & Demons
Ghosts
Historical
Horror
Humorous
Interracial
LGBT
Mystery

Paranormal
People in Uniform
Poetry
Rock Stars
Romantic Erotica
Science Fiction
Shapeshifters
Suspense
Thrillers
Urban
Vampires
Victorian
Werewolves
Westerns

FANTASY

Angels

Crime Fiction—Heist

Devils & Demons

Dragons

Elves & Fae

Ghosts

Gods & Goddesses

Horror

Psychics

Metaphysical & Visionary

Arthurian

Norse & Viking

Superhero

Sword & Sorcery

Humor

Mystery

Non-Romantic

Romantic

Thriller

Vampires

Werewolves & Shifters

Witches & Wizards

HEALTH, FITNESS & DIETING

Ab Workouts

Addiction

Alternative Therapies

Alzheimer's Disease

Antioxidants & Phytochemicals

Anxieties & Phobias

Asthma

Attention-Deficit Disorder

Autism & Asperger's Syndrome

Backache

Behavior

Bipolar Disorder

Blood Type Diets

Caffeine

Cancer—Bone Cancer

Cancer—Brain Cancer

Cancer—Breast Cancer

Cancer—Colorectal Cancer

Cancer—Leukemia

Cancer—Lung Cancer

Cancer—Lymphatic Cancer

Cancer—Prostate Disease

Cancer—Skin Cancer

Cancer Prevention

Candida

Chronic Fatigue Syndrome

Chronic Pain

Cognitive Behavioral Therapy

Cognitive Neuroscience

Contagious Diseases

Cystic Fibrosis

Developmental Psychology

Dissociative Identity

Down Syndrome

Eating Disorders

Endocrine System

Endometriosis

Energy Healing

Epilepsy

Ethnopsychology

Fiber

Food Additives

Food Allergies

For Children

For the Aging

Gambling

Genetically Engineered Food

Gluten Free

Grief & Loss

Group Therapy

Hair Loss

Headaches

Hepatitis

High Blood Pressure

Hip & Thigh Workouts

Hoarding

Hypnosis for Diets

Injuries & Rehabilitation

Irritable Bowel Syndrome

Learning Disorders

Lice

Longevity

Low Carb

Low Cholesterol

Lupus

Men's Style

Movements

Multiple Sclerosis

Obsessive Compulsive Disorder

Oral Health

Organ Transplants

Osteoporosis

Parkinson's Disease

Pilates

Post-Traumatic Stress Disorder

Postpartum Depression

Practice Management

Pregnancy

Prostate Health

Quick Workouts

Repetitive Strain Injury

Rheumatic Diseases

Schizophrenia

Sexual Addiction

Sexual Health & Impotence

Skin Care

Special Needs Children

Spinal Cord Injuries

Strokes

Swimming

Thyroid Conditions

Tobacco

Tourette's Syndrome

Triathlons

Ulcers & Gastritis

Vegan

Vegetarian

Walking

Wheat Free

Work-Related Health

HISTORY

Ancient—Aztec
Ancient—Incan
Ancient—Mesopotamia
Ancient—Prehistory
Canada—First Nations
Canada—Province & Local
Military—Regiments
Religion—Christianity
Science & Medicine
Social Gay & Gender Studies
Social Labor & Workforce
Social Race & Ethnicity
United States—Civil War
United States—Immigration
Women in History

LGBT

Bisexual Romance
Fantasy
LGBT Studies
Politics
Science Fiction
Transgender Romance

MYSTERY, THRILLER & SUSPENSE

Amateur Sleuth
Assassinations
Beaches
British Detectives
Conspiracies
Cozy—Animals
Cozy—Crafts & Hobbies
Cozy—Culinary
Crime Fiction—English
Crime Fiction—Heist
Crime Fiction—Murder
Crime Fiction—Noir
Crime Fiction—Northern Irish
Crime Fiction—Organized Crime
Crime Fiction—Scandinavian
Crime Fiction—Scottish
Crime Fiction—Serial Killers
Crime Fiction—Vigilante Justice
Crime Fiction—Welsh
Dark
Disturbing
FBI Agents
Female Protagonists
Financial
Fun
General Paranormal
Humorous
Islands
Mountains
Outer Space

Paranormal—Psychics
Paranormal—Vampires
Paranormal—Werewolves & Shifters
Police Officers
Private Investigators
Pulp
Racy

Scary
Small Towns
Suburban
Terrorism
Urban
Vengeful

RELIGION & SPIRITUALITY

Bibles—More Translations
Catholicism
Christian Fiction—Poetry
Christian Living
Earth-Based Religions—Druidism
Hebrew Bible (Old Testament)
History—Historical Jesus
Islam
Judaism—Hasidism
New Age
Occult—Alchemy
Occult—Ghosts & Haunted Houses
Occult—Metaphysical Phenomena

Other Eastern Religions
Protestantism—Inspirational
Protestantism—Self-Help
Religion & Spirituality
Spirituality—Gifts
Spirituality—Inspirational
Spirituality—Personal Growth
Spirituality—Women
Theology—Catholic
Theology—Creationism
Theology—Prophecy
Worship & Devotion

ROMANCE

Amnesia
Beaches
Cowboy
Doctor
Firefighter
Gambling & Poker
General
Highlander

Inspirational Amish
Inspirational General
International
Love Triangle
Medical
Military
Multicultural & Interracial
New Adult & College

Paranormal—Angels
Paranormal—Demons & Devils
Paranormal—Ghosts
Paranormal—Psychics
Paranormal—Vampires
Paranormal—Werewolves & Shifters
Paranormal—Witches & Wizards
Pirate
Political
Rich & Wealthy

Romantic Comedy
Royalty & Aristocrats
Second Chances
Secret Baby
Sports
Spy
Vacation
Viking
Wedding
Workplace

SCIENCE FICTION

AIs
Alien Invasion
Aliens
Clones
Colonization
Corporations
Cyberpunk
First Contact
Galactic Empire

Genetic Engineering
Metaphysical & Visionary
Mutants
Pirates
Psychics
Robots & Androids
Space Exploration
Space Fleet
Space Marine

TRAVEL

Air Travel
Alabama
Arkansas
Australia
Bosnia & Herzegovina
California
Croatia
England
Illinois

Indonesia
Italy
London
Louisiana
Motorcycle Travel
Nepal
Nevada
New York
New Zealand

North & South Korea
Northern Ireland
Philippines
Scotland
Singapore
Solo Travel

Thailand
Travel with Pets
United States
Vietnam
Wales

YOUNG ADULT AND TEEN

Angels & Demons
Detectives
Fantasy—Coming of Age
Ghosts
Mystery—Fantasy & Supernatural
Mystery—Romantic
Mystery—Science Fiction
Mystery—Spies
Romance—Fantasy & Paranormal
Romance—Historical

Science Fiction & Dystopian
Science Fiction—Action & Adventure
Science Fiction—Aliens
Science Fiction—Time Travel
Sword & Sorcery
Vampires
Werewolves & Shifters
Witches & Wizards
Zombies

LAST WORDS FOR ASPIRING & CAREER AUTHORS

At some point in his or her life, every writer has dreamed of being published and sharing this passion with others. As writers, whether published or working toward publication, we want to get what is in our heads onto paper or on the screen. It is something we need to do in order to fulfill goals, desires, and dreams.

This takes work. Lots and lots of work. Few writers can pour out everything in their heads and hearts and become published without truly learning the craft. It can take a relatively short time toward publication or it can take years, depending on your process and the aspects of your life that are uniquely your own.

If you don't have a lot of time to devote to your craft, set a goal of doing one writing-related thing every day. Read a chapter in a book on writing, do an internet search on a topic you're interested in, or work on a character profile. Best of all, write. Get in the habit of doing at least some small thing daily and it will become easier and a part of you.

When it comes to writing, get something down on paper or in a doc on your computer. Anything is better than nothing. Remember these key points:

- There is no such thing as perfection. If you try to make everything you write perfect from the start, you will get stuck and never get past that point.

- Don't edit and re-edit your first chapter over and over. Use the comments function in Word as you go, or write a list of things on a notepad, or put ideas in a separate document as you think of them. You can backfill these items during your second draft.

- You can't edit a blank page, so keep on writing and don't let anything stop you.

- Be disciplined and protect your writing time. This is your time to create or do something writing-related.

- Learn to say "NO." Don't let others think that because you're a writer and you work at home you have extra time to devote to outside activities.

- Treat writing as a career. When you work at a day job, your employer expects you to be at your desk at a certain time every day. Do the same for your career as a writer. Even get out of your pajamas and get ready for the day before you sit down at your PC.

Most importantly, enjoy your writing career. You are doing something that impacts hundreds, thousands, or even millions of people. You have the power to make a difference in someone else's life.

As a fiction author, you take readers to another world and allow them a vacation from their everyday lives. You give them a reprieve from stress and illness. Some readers are housebound or bedridden, but they can still read, and they live for some new way to break free of their confines for as long as your book lasts.

Even after the final word in the final chapter, your reader will reflect on what he or she has read. Your words will live on.

ABOUT THE AUTHORS

CHEYENNE MCCRAY

Cheyenne McCray fell in love with reading and writing from a young age--she decided in kindergarten that one day she would become an author. Thirty years later, that's exactly what she did. Today, Chey is an award-winning *New York Times* and *USA Today* bestselling fiction author with a twenty-year career as both a traditionally and indie published author, and she has written over fifty published novels and over fifty published novellas. Millions of her books have sold worldwide in print and ebook. Cheyenne has been traditionally and indie published in romantic suspense, suspense with romantic elements, contemporary romance, paranormal romance, and urban fantasy. She has given countless workshops, been on numerous panels, taken many classes, and has attended multiple conferences and conventions. She is currently writing a cozy mystery series to be launched under the name Deb Ries. Visit her website at www.CheyenneMcCray.com.

H. D. THOMSON

After working in the corporate world as an accountant, H.D. Thomson changed her focus to one of her passions—books. She owned and operated an online bookstore for several years and fell in love with the written word and started writing soon after graduating from the University of Arizona. Now she has a twenty-year career, and writes romantic suspense, paranormal and contemporary romance. She loves writing about tortured heroes and ordinary people placed in extraordinary circumstances. Her books have won and finaled in numerous writing competitions, including the RWA's Golden

Heart, Suzannah and Emily contests. H.D. owns and operates Bella Media Management. The company specializes in websites, video trailers, eBook conversion and promotional resources for authors and small businesses. She loves working with fellow writers and knows how tough the publishing industry is personally. You can find H.D. at http://www.hdthomson.com and https://bellamediamanagement.com

Made in the USA
Coppell, TX
05 August 2021